OF MYTHS & STICKS

Eddie Shore indirectly caused the first NHL All-Star game. Shore hit "Ace" Bailey so badly that it was expected that Bailey would die. Then Toronto (who Bailey played for) played against a team made up of the other NHL players in a charity game as a fundraiser for Bailey. Thus the first NHL All-Star game was born. PHOTO: COURTESY OF THE BOSTON PUBLIC LIBRARY, LESLIE JONES COLLECTION

It's time to put on our Sherlock Holmes–style thinking caps (what were they called—deerstalkers?) and look at some interesting tales that most hockey fans may think they know but probably don't know completely.

Switching momentarily from a deerstalker to a fedora, Indiana Jones said that archaeology is the search for fact. That's what I'm here for, looking for facts. Anything else you're looking for, Indiana Jones mentioned something about a philosophy class down the hall.

Every day at work I put together statistics and information to make our hockey programs better. I always seem to discover things that could be considered "myth busters" or something you thought you knew but actually didn't know. There are a lot of myths and urban legends in the hockey world; this book will, hopefully, debunk and set the record straight on many of those stories.

Author Brad Meltzer had a TV show on the History Channel called *Decoded*. The premise of the show is to look at historical events and from a different perspective, something beyond the obvious, and beyond what folklore tells us. I seek to do something similar in this book. (I also do it at TSN on a daily basis—where's *my* TV show?) I've put together some stories from the history of hockey; I've analyzed them, researched and uncovered some facts that will hopefully change your way of thinking about them.

As Joe Friday said—what is it about fedoras?— "Just the facts."

1

OLD-TIME HOCKEY

AH YES, YESTERYEAR IN THE NHL, WHEN YOU COULD BLACKEN an eye and bruise a thigh and get away with it because there was no video, no social media, one referee and a beating was generally accepted as part of the evening.

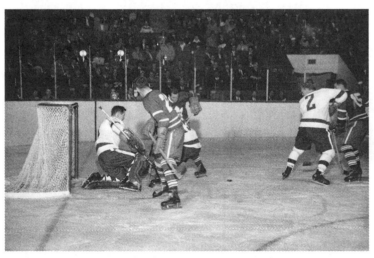

The Leafs and Wings battle for the vulcanized rubber. Once upon a time a cow's knee was used as a puck. PHOTO: CITY OF TORONTO ARCHIVES, FONDS 1257, SERIES 1057, ITEM 7526

WHERE AND WHEN IT ALL BEGAN

EVERYONE WANTS TO KNOW THE BASICS: WHEN WAS THE FIRST National Hockey League game? Who scored the first goal? Was there a 50/50 draw that night? Important historical information. The first NHL games took place on Tuesday December 19, 1917. The Montreal Canadiens defeated the Ottawa Senators 7–4 in Ottawa and in the other game of the day, the Montreal Wanderers came out ahead of the Toronto Arenas 10–9 in an opening-night shootout in La Belle Province. It would be the only game that the Wanderers would ever win. Here are the box scores from those games.

CANADIENS 7 SENATORS 4

PERIOD	TEAM	GOAL SCORER	ASSIST
1	MTL	Joe Malone (1)	
1	MTL	Newsy Lalonde (1)	
1	MTL	Joe Malone (2)	Didier Pitre
2	OTT	Eddie Gerard (1)	Cy Denneny
2	MTL	Joe Malone (3)	Joe Hall
2	MTL	Joe Malone (4)	Joe Hall
2	OTT	Cy Denneny (1)	
2	OTT	Cy Denneny (2)	
3	MTL	Joe Malone (5)	Newsy Lalonde
3	MTL	Didier Pitre (1)	Jack Laviolette
3	OTT	Cy Denneny (3)	Hamby Shore

OFFICIALS: Harvey Pulford and Charlie McKinley
BETWEEN THE PIPES: MTL—Georges Vezina, OTT—Clint Benedict

This game also gave us our first NHL labour holdouts. Hamby Shore and Jack Darragh refused to play the first period for Ottawa in a contract dispute. They both sat on the bench for the opening session. During the intermission they worked out their contracts with management and eventually took to the ice. Since the score was 3–0 for Montreal at the end of the first period, and they had Georges Vezina in net and not to mention the "trap," even Darragh and Shore couldn't bring the Senators back to get the victory. Hamby Shore is no relation to Eddie Shore. Hamby was short for Hamilton, but Shore was not from the Golden Horseshoe— Hamilton was merely his middle name. He was born and raised in Ottawa.

A morbid note of interest about two players in this game: Hamby Shore died before the start of the 1918–19 season from the flu epidemic. Montreal's Joe Hall died at the end of the 1919 season, also from the flu. The epidemic led to the cancellation of the 1919 Stanley Cup Final between the Montreal Canadiens and the Seattle Metropolitans.

WANDERERS 10   ARENAS 9

PERIOD	TEAM	GOAL SCORER	ASSIST
1	MTL	Dave Ritchie (1)	
1	MTL	Jack McDonald (1)	
1	TOR	Reg Noble (1)	
1	TOR	Harry Cameron (1)	
1	MTL	Harry Hyland (1)	
1	MTL	Harry Hyland (2)	
2	TOR	Alf Skinner (1)	
2	MTL	Harry Hyland (3)	
2	TOR	Corbett Denneny (1)	
2	TOR	Reg Noble (2)	
2	MTL	Billy Bell (1)	
2	MTL	Art Ross (1)	
2	MTL	Harry Hyland (4)	
3	MTL	Dave Ritchie (2)	
3	TOR	Reg Noble (3)	
3	TOR	Corbett Denneny (2)	
3	TOR	Reg Noble (4)	

OFFICIALS: Lt. Tom Melville (no relation to Lt. Dan from *Forrest Gump*) and Jack Marshall
BETWEEN THE PIPES: TOR—Sammy Hebert, MTL—Bert Lindsay

ORIGINAL SIX?

WHEN THE MAPLE LEAFS, CANADIENS, BLACKHAWKS, RED Wings, Bruins and Rangers are mentioned, it is usually followed by the term "Original Six." But of those six teams, only *two* are original, and of those two, only one has kept the same name.

When the NHL launched in December 1917, it was comprised of four teams: Montreal Canadiens, Toronto Arenas (changed to St. Patricks in 1919 then to Maple Leafs in 1927), Montreal Wanderers and the Ottawa Senators. These were not the Senators we know

A 1964 game between Toronto and Montreal. The Leafs defeated the Habs in seven games in round one of the playoffs on their way to winning the Stanley Cup over Detroit. PHOTO: LIBRARY AND ARCHIVES CANADA/CREDIT: LOUIS JAQUES/WEEKEND MAGAZINE FONDS/E002505696

The Rangers and Habs only met once in the Stanley Cup Final. In 1979, the Canadiens won in five games. PHOTO: LIBRARY AND ARCHIVES CANADA/ CREDIT: LOUIS JAQUES/WEEKEND MAGAZINE FONDS/E002505707

today; the previous version left Ottawa in 1934 to become the St. Louis Eagles and were defunct after one season. I guess St. Louis was the Gateway to Hockey Bankruptcy back then.

This leaves us with Toronto and Montreal. Toronto's team was originally called the Arenas and they were referred to as the "Blueshirts," a nickname later adopted, of course, by the New York Rangers (I guess because when Toronto switched to the St. Patricks they weren't blue anymore and the nickname was available).

Technically the Montreal Canadiens are the only original, originally named team in the NHL. The more accurate term for the Original Six would be the "Last Six." It's not like the other four teams came in together and joined only Toronto and Montreal. There were ten teams (Bruins, Leafs, Canadiens, Rangers, Cougars, Pirates, Maroons, Black Hawks, Senators, Americans) in the NHL for many years before they were trimmed down to six in 1942–43. The Bruins came into the league in 1924, the Rangers and Blackhawks in 1926 and the Red Wings in 1932. Detroit, like

Toronto, had a couple of name changes: Cougars to Falcons to Red Wings—and the Red Wings name came from a junior team in Montreal.

Depending on your point of view you can go with the Last Six or Original Four and we go with different teams, and either is fine with me. And hopefully we will stop hearing about an "Original Six match-up" every time Montreal plays, say, Chicago.

TRADER VIC

Left-winger Vic Lynn was traded five times and he played for all six so-called Original Six teams between 1942 and 1954. That's quite the feat. When you pro-rate to today's terms, he would have played for all 30 teams and been traded 20 times, take that Mike Sillinger, traded nine times!

Lynn's first three stops were as easy as one-two-three—as in the games played with the Rangers (one), Red Wings (three) and Canadiens (two). Then he played over 200 with Toronto, 68 with Boston and finally 40 with Chicago. I wonder if he took the hint and became a real estate agent during one of the off-seasons to save on money.

Vic Lynn was born on January 26, same as Wayne Gretzky. So they have that and their alumni Rangers status in common, if one game gets Lynn on the invite list.

50/50 DRAW

MAURICE RICHARD WAS THE FIRST PLAYER IN NHL HISTORY TO score 50 goals in 50 games. He did so in the 1944–45 season. Let's go back a couple of years to Richard's rookie season in 1942–43. Richard picked up his first point in his first career game, just 36 seconds into the Halloween 1942 contest against the Bruins. It was an assist on a goal by Tony Demers. Demers would only score one more goal in his NHL career and that came in the second period of that game. Demers is known for two things in his career, 1) scoring a goal to give "The Rocket" his first NHL point and 2) being convicted of manslaughter in September 1949 for killing his girlfriend. He was sentenced to 16 years and served six.

In 1944–45, Maurice Richard became the first player to score 50 goals in 50 games. PHOTO: LIBRARY AND ARCHIVES CANADA/THOMAS PATRICK GORMAN FONDS/E000943076

AN AWARDING EXPERIENCE

HERE IS SOME BACKGROUND INFORMATION ON A FEW ANNUAL hockey awards that I find mildly amusing. Meaning some of them don't make any sense...

The **LESTER PATRICK TROPHY** is awarded for contributions to hockey in the United States. Lester Patrick was a Canadian from Quebec and spent some time at the family lumberyard in B.C. before making his mark in the NHL. After retiring he settled in Victoria, B.C. Patrick put the *eh* in U.S. *eh*.

The **VEZINA TROPHY** goes to the season's best goalie in the league. Georges Vezina was a legendary Canadiens goalie in the early years of the NHL. He had 24 children. He was known for saves on the ice and scoring off. Yes, I basically put this award reference in the book for that joke alone. I mean come on, 24 kids, wow.

The **ART ROSS TROPHY** is awarded to the player who leads the league in scoring at season's end. Ross had one point in his entire NHL career. Wow, what an ego. The NHL owners back in the '40s named many of the league awards after themselves or after NHL front-office employees.

And now a couple of awards named after players, who unfortunately had to die to have awards named after them ...

The **BILL MASTERTON MEMORIAL TROPHY** is given annually to the NHL player who best exemplifies the qualities of perseverance, sportsmanship and dedication to hockey. Bill Masterton is the only player to die of injuries suffered in an NHL game. On Saturday January 13, 1968, in a game against the California Seals in Minnesota, North Stars forward Masterton was bodychecked by Ron Harris and then bounced off of Larry Cahan at the Seals blue line. Masterton's head hit the ice and started bleeding. Minnesota coach Wren Blair believed that Masterton was out cold before he hit the ice. Masterton had been suffering from concussion-like symptoms since he was knocked groggy by a hit during a game against Boston on December 30. Since that game, Masterton had

Georges Vezina was Montreal's best goalie. PHOTO: MONTREAL LA PRESSE/
THE CANADIAN PRESS

been complaining of headaches and missed some practice time
because of it. Masterton also had been vomiting quite frequently
but it was thought he just had the flu. The fatal incident occurred in
the first period. The game ended in a tie, 2–2. Masterton, who was a
career minor leaguer until the 1967 expansion, scored the first goal
in North Stars history against St. Louis in the franchise's first-ever

game. That game also ended tied at 2. Masterton's first and last NHL games had the same score. After the January 13 game, Masterton was taken to Fairview Southdale Hospital in Edina, Minnesota. He never regained consciousness. Five neurosurgeons examined Masterton and they ruled out operating on him. Masterton died at 1:55 a.m. on January 15 from a massive brain injury.

The **HOBEY BAKER AWARD** goes to the top player of the season in NCAA Hockey. I thought I would segue from Masterton to Hobey Baker, because Masterton died on Baker's birthday. Hobey Baker was born on January 15, 1892. Although Baker never played in the NHL, he still had an interesting hockey career. Baker was a two-sport athlete at Princeton: football and hockey. He was good enough to captain both squads. Baker was also a classmate of Jazz Age novelist F. Scott Fitzgerald (the character Allenby in *This Side of Paradise* is supposedly based on Baker). Baker gave up hockey to be a pilot in World War I, during which he shot down several German planes. He was named captain yet again—this time of the 141st Aero Squadron, AEF. Baker got through the battles without a scratch. But just before he was to return home, he was test-piloting a repaired plane in Toul, France when it crashed, killing Baker. He was just 26 years old. Baker died on the exact day that season two of the NHL started.

WHO IS THAT MASKED MAN?

CANADIENS NETMINDER JACQUES PLANTE DEFINITELY WORE a mask, and he was the first goalie to wear one full-time. That's the proper qualifying term: "full-time." Montreal Maroons goalie Clint Benedict wore a mask in an NHL game 30 years before Plante did, though. So if you are ever asked who the first NHL goalie to wear a mask was, the answer is Benedict, not Plante. Benedict was hit in the face by a Howie Morenz shot, breaking his nose. Benedict returned to the net a few weeks later with a mask. He used it for a few games but he had trouble seeing down and ceased using the mask.

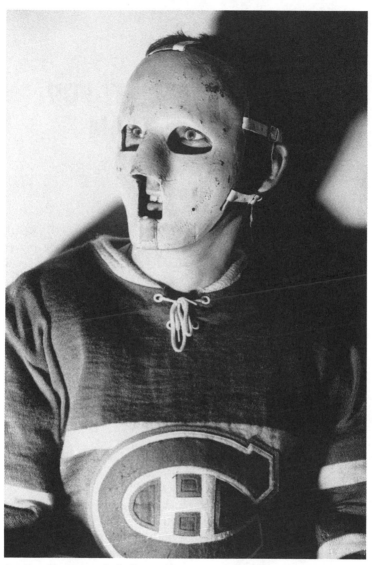

Jacques Plante wasn't the first goalie to wear a mask. He was technically the first goalie to wear a plastic one. PHOTO: AP/THE CANADIAN PRESS

2

ROOT, ROOT, ROOT FOR THE HOME TEAM

JERRY SEINFELD ONCE SAID THAT, WHEN CHEERING FOR YOUR team, you are basically rooting for laundry. If your favourite player leaves the team, he no longer wears the clothes that you cheer for. Consider this chapter a guide for helping you sort your NHL laundry.

REPRESENTING

SO HOW MANY TEAMS HAVE PLAYED IN THE NHL? THAT WOULD be 48. Here is some background information—and trivia, of course—on when each team started and, in some cases, when they ceased to be. If you're going to cheer on your team, it's best to know their history, right?

MONTREAL CANADIENS (1917–present): Many people think that the *H* in the team logo stands for "Habs." It doesn't. It stands for "Hockey" as in the Canadiens Hockey Club. Montreal has won twenty Stanley Cups; no other franchise is within ten of them. That is one NHL record that will be hard to beat. Canadiens goalie Georges Vezina recorded the first shutout in NHL history in 1918 when Montreal beat the Arenas in Toronto 9–0. The Canadiens led 1–0 at the end of the first period, then they lit up Harry Holmes for six in the second period and that's all she wrote. Montreal had

"Toe" Blake won three Stanley Cups as a player and eight as a coach, all with the Montreal Canadiens. PHOTO: LIBRARY AND ARCHIVES CANADA/ CREDIT: LOUIS JAQUES/WEEKEND MAGAZINE FONDS/E002505697

the first-ever linemates inducted into the Hockey Hall of Fame. Rocket Richard, Elmer Lach and Toe Blake—together known as the "Punch Line"—were all inducted in 1966.

TORONTO ARENAS (1917–20): In December of 1919 the Arenas were sold to the group that owned the St. Patricks of the OHA, thus the name change to the **ST. PATS** in 1920. Seven years later they became the **MAPLE LEAFS** (1927–present). Toronto businessman Conn Smythe, who bought the team after the New York Rangers fired him as GM over a difference of opinion on what players to sign, changed the name to something he thought as more patriotic. He said that the blue and white colours came from the Canadian blue skies and the white snow. (This makes Toronto the only team in NHL history to change its name during the season.) The Maple Leafs played their first game on February 17, 1927, in which they defeated the New York Americans 4–1. George Patterson scored the first-ever goal in Maple Leafs history. He was just dealt to the team two weeks earlier and had never played an NHL game before. Patterson was from Kingston, which should make Don Cherry happy. The Maple Leafs were almost sold for $4 million in 1958 to the Regency hotel chain. They were going to change the team name again to the Rockets, but, of course, didn't. Corb Denneny is the only player to play for all three Toronto teams.

Toronto celebrates a goal. The 1942 Maple Leafs was the first team to win a series after trailing 3–0. PHOTO: ARCHIVES OF ONTARIO F 223-3-2-7-5

OTTAWA SENATORS (1917–31): The original Senators took a year off and returned for the 1932–33 season. Then in the following season the franchise became the **ST. LOUIS EAGLES** (1934–35). The Eagles lasted just one season and the franchise folded. The day the Senators moved to St. Louis the NHL implemented the penalty-shot rule. The penalty shot was invented by the Patrick brothers in the Pacific Coast Hockey Association. The Senators won four Stanley Cups from 1919–27. In 1930, Ottawa traded arguably their best player in King Clancy to the Leafs for $35,000 and two players. Clancy retired from play in 1936 as the NHL's highest-scoring defencemen. Perhaps there is a "Curse of the King" in Ottawa, as the Senators have not only not won a Cup since the trade, they have also never defeated the Leafs in a playoff series.

The original Ottawa Senators played in the NHL for 16 seasons before moving to St. Louis for one season in 1934–35. PHOTO: LIBRARY AND ARCHIVES CANADA/E006608843

MONTREAL WANDERERS (1917–18): The Wanderers were the English team in Montreal. Their two star players from the NHA days, Odie and Sprague Cleghorn, had to sit out the season due to a wartime exemption. Missing those two players was hard on the team in its first NHL season. The Wanderers pleaded with league officials to provide them with players from the other three teams in the NHL or they would quit the league. On January 2, 1918, the NHL was going to hold a meeting to determine whether or not they could provide players to the Montreal club. Before a decision was made, the Montreal Arena burnt to the ground. Rather than play their home games at the Jubilee Rink in the French part of Montreal, the Wanderers folded and their players dispersed. The Wanderers were to host the Canadiens on January 2 and the Wanderers were in last place in the NHL with one win in six games. Their top scorer was Harry Hyland with six goals; he was seventh in the league in scoring at the time of the fire. That's interesting: Rink burns to the ground, when the team was threatening to quit the league, and on the day the NHL had a meeting to discuss giving Montreal extra players. Talk about a bad luck day. I wonder what CSI: Montreal turned up in the fire investigation?

QUEBEC BULLDOGS (1919–20): The Bulldogs were, for all intents and purposes, the first expansion team in NHL history as they joined the pro league in its third season. The Bulldogs had the Good, the Bad and the Ugly. The Good was Joe Malone, arguably the NHL's greatest goal scorer. And he didn't disappoint in 1919–20, scoring 39 goals in 24 games and picking up the Art Ross Trophy. The Bad: the rest of the team totaled 42 goals. A quick math lesson tells us the Bulldogs didn't do too well when 90 percent of their goals came from one player. Then we have an English lesson to back that up in the form of the word "Holes" which was the nickname of the Quebec goalie. When you're a goalie, is it possible to have a worse nickname then "Holes"? I don't think so. That would be the Ugly.

The Bulldogs then became the **HAMILTON TIGERS** (1920–25). The change of location didn't help the franchise that much in the first four seasons—they dwelled in the cellar each year. Then in

1924–25, under the guidance of coach Art Ross, the Tigers finished first. This was quite impressive since the league had added two more teams by then. Before they could pop the champagne in Hamilton and celebrate, something was a little off. The NHL had increased the games played in 1924–25 from 24 to 30. The Tigers players' contracts remained the same. The players figured they were owed $200 each for the extra six games played. During the semifinal series between Toronto and Montreal, the Tigers presented an ultimatum to GM Percy Thompson. Pay or no play. Tigers threatened to skip the finals if they weren't paid. Sounds similar to the issues that baseball's 1919 Chicago White Sox had with Charlie Comiskey. The Tigers didn't get a chance to play in the final as they were suspended by NHL President Frank Calder and in an interesting turn of events, they were each fined $200. That was it for the Hamilton franchise. One regular season title and Billy Burch won the Hart Trophy. The franchise moved to New York on November 7, 1925.

NEW YORK AMERICANS (1925–41): In seventeen seasons, the Americans finished above .500 just three times. No Stanley Cup or league titles. The Americans didn't entirely live up to their team nickname, either: they had just one American-born player on their team in season one. Bob Hall was born in Illinois and played his junior hockey in Brooklyn. He played eight games with the Americans, and that was it for his NHL career. In 1928–29 Americans goalie Roy Worters became the first goaltender in NHL history to win the Hart Trophy. Not bad for a guy who refused to play for the Americans a year earlier and was suspended by the league. The franchise's final season was in 1941–42 when they became the **BROOKLYN AMERICANS**, though they never actually played a game in Brooklyn. The team instead rented Manhattan's Madison Square Garden for home games.

MONTREAL MAROONS (1924–38): Sometimes the team was referred to as the Millionaires, which was a popular nickname for pro and amateur teams in the early part of the century. The Maroons hold a few distinctions: they were the last team to win the Stanley Cup when it was awarded to the winner of an interleague show-down. Montreal won it in 1926 defeating Lester Patrick's Victoria Cougars of the Western Hockey League. They were also the last so-called non–Original Six team to win the cup (1935) until the Philadelphia Flyers won in 1974. The Montreal Forum was built in 1924 for the Maroons but when the Great Depression eventually forced the end of their tenure, the Habs took over as sole occupant. While at the Forum the Maroons hosted the longest NHL game ever put to the ice. The game, against the Detroit Red Wings, started at 8:30 p.m. on March 24, 1936 and ended at 2:24 a.m. on March 25, 1936. In NHL time, the game lasted 176 minutes and 30 seconds, just a few minutes short of a triple-header. The final score was 1–0, with the game-winning goal scored by a rookie playing in his first ever playoff game. Detroit's Modere "Mud" Bruneteau put the winner past Lorne Chabot. Norm Smith picked up the shutout. The shots on goal were 90–67 for Montreal.

The Montreal Maroons were the third Montreal-based NHL team and the second to win a Stanley Cup. PHOTO: COURTESY OF THE BOSTON PUBLIC LIBRARY, LESLIE JONES COLLECTION

The Montreal Maroons would lose their 1929-30 playoff series 3–1 to the Bruins. Two of the games went to at least double OT. PHOTO: COURTESY OF THE BOSTON PUBLIC LIBRARY, LESLIE JONES COLLECTION

BOSTON BRUINS (1924–present): The six-time Stanley Cup winning franchise got off to a slow start in year one. They won just six games out of thirty and they scored just 49 goals while giving up 119 which was nearly double the league average. Jimmy Herberts had 17 of the 49 goals; no one else on the team had more than 5. The first NHL game outside of Canada was held in Boston. The Bruins took on the Maroons and defeated them 2–1 on December 21, 1924. Owner Charlie Adams wanted to name the team after a wild animal that displayed speed and agility. Coach Art Ross suggested the name Bruins, an old-fashioned word for "bear." The colours of the jerseys came from the chain of grocery stores that Adams owned. (Speaking of family businesses: Adams' son Weston would one day be responsible for signing franchise legend Bobby Orr.) There have only been two instances in which an NHL playoff game was not completed, and both involved the Bruins. I'm sure most hockey fans remember the fog-out in Boston against the

Oilers in 1988. The other occurred in the 1951 semifinals: the Bruins won Game One at Toronto, Game Two was tied 1–1 as the clock struck midnight and Saturday night turned into Sunday morning. Toronto law prohibited any games being played after 12 a.m. on a Saturday. The game remained tied after eighty minutes. It was never completed. Toronto would win the next four games to win the series. Three of the games were played in Boston. Having not won a Cup since 1972, the Bruins finally ended their Cup drought in 2011 when they came from being down three games to two and winning the Stanley Cup in Game Seven in Vancouver.

This photo shows a Bruins team practice in the early years of the NHL. Boston once used a Baptist minister in net for a game in 1943. PHOTO: COURTESY OF THE BOSTON PUBLIC LIBRARY, LESLIE JONES COLLECTION

PITTSBURGH PIRATES (1925–30): I wonder if the Pirates ever wore puffy shirts. The hockey team was in fact named for the baseball team. (And five years after the Pirates hockey team was no more, Babe Ruth hit the last three home runs of his career against baseball's Pittsburgh Pirates.) No Stanley Cups or first place finishes for the NHL's Pirates. They do have a place in the NHL record book however: Boxing Day, 1925 at the new Madison Square Garden,141 shots on net were taken (73 by the Americans and 68 by Pittsburgh), a league record that still stands. New York won the game 3–1. Scoring in the game: for the Pirates: Lionel Conacher, then the league's highest-paid player. For the Americans: Shorty Green, Billy Burch and Alex McKinnon. McKinnon left the game after he took a two-hander across the forehead from Hib Milks. Jake Forbes was between the pipes for the Americans and Roy "Shrimp" Worters was in net for Pittsburgh. So you had Shorty scoring on Shrimp. Worters earned the nickname because he was only five-foot-three—the shortest player in NHL history.

The Pirates franchise was supposed to move temporarily to Philadelphia as they waited for a new arena to be built in Pittsburgh (some things never change). Here they were known as the **PHILADELPHIA QUAKERS** (1930–31), named for the religious movement also known as the "Society of Friends." Pennsylvania was known as the Quaker Province from 1681–1776. The Depression, and the fact that the team itself was terrible, second worst in NHL history, caused the Pennsylvania team(s) to fold.

NEW YORK RANGERS (1926–present): The Blue Shirts have captured the Stanley Cup four times. The most recent in 1994. Madison Square Garden, where the Rangers have made their home since 1926, was originally built for the New York Americans. There have been four different arenas named Madison Square Garden. There was a belief that the Rangers were cursed from 1940–94 because Rangers management burned the mortgage on MSG in the bowl of the Stanley Cup in 1940—Rangers didn't win a cup for another 54 years. Another interesting story from Manhattan: the entire Rangers team was placed on waivers at the same time in October

Lester Patrick (wearing the suit) had to come off the bench and exchange the suit for goalie equipment during the 1928 Stanley Cup final against the Maroons. PHOTO: COURTESY OF THE BOSTON PUBLIC LIBRARY, LESLIE JONES COLLECTION

of 1975. Also, the Rangers have won 25 games on Christmas Day, which is more than any other team in the NHL. At one point the Rangers went on a 17–3 run on December 25. The NHL hasn't played on Christmas Day in over 20 years.

CHICAGO BLACK HAWKS (1926–86)/**BLACKHAWKS** (1986–present): The name Black Hawks came from the owner, Frederic McLaughlin, who in World War I belonged to a machine gun battalion named the 86th Infantry Blackhawk Division. His wife designed the team logo. For years the name was spelled as two words, however, in 1986 it was discovered that the name was actually spelled as one word when the team first came into existence.

I know the common saying is "why so serious?" How about "why so angry?" Hawks' legend Stan Mikita finished in the top 10 in penalty minutes five times and then won the Lady Byng in back

"Blackhawks" was spelt "Black Hawks" for a while until someone discovered the spelling mistake. The Black Hawks won their first Stanley Cup in 1933-34. The Blackhawks won theirs in 2009-10. PHOTO: COURTESY OF THE BOSTON PUBLIC LIBRARY, LESLIE JONES COLLECTION

to back seasons 1966–67 and 1967–68. I guess Mikita answered his own question—why so angry? Lighten up! Can't score from the penalty box. Mikita also won the Art Ross the same two years as Lady Byng, only player to do that. Hey badda-boom, badda-Byng.

DETROIT COUGARS (1926–30): The name Cougars came from the defunct Victoria team of the Western Hockey League. In year one, Detroit played in Windsor, Ontario. In an interesting move, the team changed its name from the Cougars to the **DETROIT FALCONS** (1930–32) because fans found it too hard to say "Cougars." Agricultural businessman James Norris took over ownership in 1932 and renamed the team **DETROIT RED WINGS** (1932–present) for a club he played for in Montreal called the Winged Wheelers.

The franchise didn't win any cups until they became the Red Wings. The Wings have won eleven Cups, which puts them in a tie with Toronto for the second most in NHL history. After the Wings won the Cup on April 23, 1950 in OT against the Rangers, Ted Lindsay became the first player to skate around the ice with the Stanley Cup. Lindsay did it as a tribute to the fans that, in essence, paid the players' salaries. Pete Babando beat Chuck Rayner for the game winner. Babando scored twice in the game. He only scored three career playoff goals, his last two that day against the Rangers.

PHILADELPHIA FLYERS (1967–present): The Flyers were the first Stanley Cup–winning team since 1927 that wasn't from Montreal, Toronto, Chicago, Boston, Detroit or New York. The Flyers captured the trophy in 1974 and 1975. Philadelphia began play on October 11, 1967 against expansion-mates the California Seals. The Seals won 5–1. Scoring the first goal in team history was Bill Sutherland. Outside of two playoff games with Montreal in 1963, Sutherland's NHL participation was nil. In 1967, at the age of 33, the rookie-veteran—or Corporal-Captain as Captain Hawkeye Pierce would say—scored 20 goals. In 1967, the Flyers finished first in the all-expansion-team division. But they lost to the St. Louis Blues in the playoffs. Outside of the two Cup victories, the most remarkable feat in team history has to be the 35-game unbeaten streak from October 13, 1979 to January 7, 1980. The Flyers had 25 wins and 10 ties during the run. Funny that the streak was bookended by two blowouts: 9–2 to the Atlanta Flames and 7–1 to the Minnesota North Stars.

LOS ANGELES KINGS (1967–present): In their 40-year history the Kings have been a Stanley Cup participant three times, winning in 2012 over New Jersey, and in 2014 over the Rangers. (They lost to Montreal in 1993.) In 2012, the Kings were the first team in NHL history ranked eighth in their conference to go on to win the Stanley Cup. In their first season in the league, the Kings went after a couple of key parts of the Leafs' Cup-winning team from 1967. They traded for Red Kelly and made him their coach and the very next day the Kings picked up Terry Sawchuk in the expansion draft. Sawchuk lasted just one season in Los Angeles, Kelly was there for two. Also on the Kings roster in year one was Ted Irvine, the father of wrestler Chris Jericho.

ST. LOUIS BLUES (1967–present): The Blues had a great start to their franchise. They made it to the Stanley Cup Final their first three seasons. They also went 0–12 in those games. During the 1970 final series against Boston, the Blues used three goalies: Jacques Plante, Glenn Hall and Ernie Wakely. That had never been done before and was not duplicated until 2006 when the Oilers used three goalies in the Cup Final against Carolina. The 1970 Cup Final will always be remembered for something else however: the legendary picture of Bobby Orr flying through the air. The Blues have never been back to the Stanley Cup Final.

Orr scores his famous Cup-winning OT goal against St. Louis. The Bruins swept the Blues, so if Orr hadn't scored then, he had a few games to try again. PHOTO: AP-A.E. MALOOF/THE CANADIAN PRESS

MINNESOTA NORTH STARS (1967–93): Under the ownership of the Gund brothers of Cleveland, the Minnesota franchise underwent some bizarre roster moves. First the Gunds bought the team in 1978 after the NHL essentially folded the Barons. Then they wanted to move the team to the San Francisco area in the early 1990s. However, the NHL had planned on an expansion team for nearby San Jose. The Gunds bought *that* team and were allowed to take half the Minnesota team with them, which they did. Have a look at the Sharks roster in their inaugural season and you'll see a lot of players who were on the Minnesota roster in1990–91. That year the North Stars finished below .500 but made it to the Stanley Cup Final and they lost in six games to Pittsburgh. Good thing when the franchise moved to the Lone Star State they didn't have to change the name that much. The **DALLAS STARS** (1993–present) won the Stanley Cup in 1999. Some hockey fans think that Derian Hatcher was the first non-Canadian-born team captain to hoist the Stanley Cup. That's not true. Dunc Munro of the 1926 Maroons was born in Scotland, and Johnny Gottselig of the 1938 Black Hawks was a native of Russia. The first jersey number retired in Dallas was Neal Broten's #7. Broten scored the first-ever goal for the Dallas Stars. The one story that I find amazing about the Dallas Stars was from October 14, 1995: The Stars trailed Boston 5–3 in the final 50 seconds of the game. Dallas won 6–5 in regulation. In the words of Fran Tarkenton, that's incredible. Kevin Hatcher scored at 19:11, Mike Modano at 19:44 and Guy Carbonneau at 19:55. The game was in Dallas, so you know a lot of people left at 5–3 with a minute or two left to beat the traffic. What a final 49 seconds they missed.

PITTSBURGH PENGUINS (1967–present): Three times the Penguins have sipped from the Stanley Cup—in back-to-back seasons in 1990–92 and 1991–92, and again in 2009. Sid the Kid had a good eight-month stretch in 2009–10 winning a Stanley Cup in June 2009 then scoring gold-medal-winning goal in February at the 2010 Olympics. Hall of Famer Andy Bathgate scored the first goal in Penguins history, Ab McDonald and Noel Price assisted on it. It came on October 11, 1967 against Montreal. The Habs won 2–1. I

Sidney Crosby, two-time winner of the Hart Trophy. He's wearing a full shield in this picture due to a broken jaw. PHOTO: BRUCE BENNETT/ THINKSTOCK

still miss the Pittsburgh logo with the scarf around the Penguin. At the birth of the team, Pittsburgh had a name-the-team contest, but as legend has it, one of the part-owners' wives came up with the name Penguins picking up on the arena's nickname: the Big Igloo. Too bad penguins are from the South Pole and igloos are generally used in the North Pole.

CALIFORNIA (OAKLAND) SEALS (1967–70): The team started off as California, then they were, more specifically, Oakland halfway through the year. The Seals had a few owners, the original being 28-year-old Barry Van Gerbig, whose godfather was Bing Crosby. So you had your anthem singer right there. The team was sold a year later to a group that involved George Gillett, who would eventually own the Canadiens for a period of time. Two years after that, Charlie Finley, the owner of baseball's Oakland Athletics bought the team and renamed them **CALIFORNIA GOLDEN SEALS** (1970–76). He changed the team colours to resemble those of the Athletics, plus he threw in white skates, which were hand-painted by the Seals staff. The only white skates back then outside of hockey would have been those of female figure skaters. The NHL ran the team for a couple of years before local businessman Mel Swig bought the team. He planned on building a new rink with the help of the city of San Francisco but the arena was scrapped after a new mayor was elected. Minority owner George Gund (see also Minnesota North Stars) persuaded Swig to move the team to Cleveland, and they were renamed the **CLEVELAND BARONS** (1976–78). The Gund brothers bought the team from Swig after the first season in Cleveland as Swig lost a lot of money due to poor attendance. The Barons merged with Minnesota prior to the start of the 78–79 season; they kept the North Stars name and took the Barons position in the Adams Division. Now that's a nice compromise.

BUFFALO SABRES (1970–present): The only time the Sabres won a Stanley Cup was during the movie *Bruce Almighty*. Other than that, they have had two appearances in the Cup Final, both resulting in non-triumphs. In 1975 they lost in six games to the Broad Street Bullies. Then in 1999, the "No Goal" game. The Stars' Brett Hull had his foot in the crease when he scored the OT winner against the Sabres. Again Buffalo lost in six games. Jim Watson scored the first goal in Buffalo history. It was the first goal in his NHL career. Watson had a total of four NHL goals and eight WHA goals.

VANCOUVER CANUCKS (1970–present): Playing in the Stanley Cup against teams from New York is not good karma for the Canucks. They were swept in 1982 by the Islanders and then in 1994 lost in seven against Mark Messier's Rangers. Then, of course, they lost

Before the Canucks represented Vancouver in the NHL, the Millionaires were the city's team in the PCHA in the early 1900s. PHOTO: CITY OF VANCOUVER ARCHIVES, 586-4280

in seven against the Bruins in 2011. Vancouver would have their revenge on Messier. The Canucks signed him to a contract in 1997 and he would never participate in another playoff game. One of the more interesting stories in Canucks history involves Pat Quinn. Quinn was the coach of the L.A. Kings in 1986–87. His contract was up at the end of the year. On Christmas Eve, Quinn approached Vancouver about a job for the following season. The Canucks signed Quinn to become vice-president and GM of the team and they gave him a $100,000 signing bonus. The Kings were informed of the deal. Within a couple of weeks, word of the transaction leaked out from a Vancouver radio station. Quinn was suspended by the NHL for the final half of the 1986–87 season. President John Ziegler asked Vancouver to tear up the contract, but they refused.

NEW YORK ISLANDERS (1972—present): Winners of four straight Stanley Cups. The Isles kicked off their first season in the league in the basement with a 12–60–6 record. When they won their first cup, in 1980, four players remained on the roster from 1972: Billy Smith, Lorne Henning, Garry Howatt and Swedish-born Bob Nystrom. Billy Smith was always known as a fiery goaltender. However you might not expect him to pick up the franchise's first ever fighting major. Smith dropped the blocker and glove against Rod Gilbert of the Rangers. The Rangers won the game 2–1, with Gilbert picking up an assist on the Rangers' first goal.

ATLANTA FLAMES (1972–80): The Flames played their home games at The Omni. They should have named it Tara, for its similarity to that other doomed Southern structure. No Stanley Cups, no finals, no retired numbers, no Hall of Famers. It's almost like the franchise went up in Flames. Pun intended. Morris Stefaniw scored the first goal in Atlanta history. He never scored again. The franchise moved north and became the **CALGARY FLAMES** (1980–present). Stanley Cup champions in 1989 and two-time finalists. There are always criticisms of Calgary for trading Brett Hull in 1988, but the Flames won a cup after the deal with the Blues. St. Louis never won a cup.

Two teams from Atlanta moved to Canada. The Flames went to Calgary and the Thrashers moved to Winnipeg to become the Jets 2.0. PHOTO: MARIANNE HELM/THINKSTOCK

The cost to move from Atlanta to Calgary was $16 million. Wonder how much of that went to U-Haul?

WASHINGTON CAPITALS (1974–present): The Capitals' first season was also their worst—the worst in NHL history, in fact. No team has ever lost more games—67. One win on the road. Can't you just hear that motivational speaker from *The Natural*? "Losing is a disease, as contagious as syphilis." The Capitals are all over the map, literally; they used to play in Maryland, practice in Virginia, yet call D.C. home. Not to mention that Hall of Famer Rod Langway was born in Taiwan.

KANSAS CITY SCOUTS (1974–76): The team's logo was based on a statue in Kansas City that was nicknamed the Scout. The franchise's first game was in Toronto. Leafs won 6–2. Dave Keon scored his 350th career goal in the game. KC's Simon Nolet and Lynn Powis put the puck behind Leaf's goalie Doug Favell. The franchise moved two states westward and became the **COLORADO ROCKIES** (1976–82). Don Cherry, Lanny McDonald and of course Hardy Astrom, who was made famous by many rants from the Grape One, stating that Astrom was the worst goalie he ever saw and he used to fake injuries to not play. Before Astrom was in the Rockies net, there was Doug Favell—the goalie that beat the Scouts in their first-ever game. The goalie that won the Rockies first game was Doug Favell, against the Leafs. Moving back east, the franchise became the **NEW JERSEY DEVILS** (1982–present), named for a legendary creature—the Jersey Devil—that supposedly prowled the Pine Barrens of southern New Jersey. After a 13–4 loss at the hands of Edmonton in 1983, Wayne Gretzky called the organization "Mickey Mouse." New Jersey has since won three Stanley Cups. I wonder if the players went to Disney World afterward to meet Mickey Mouse. On April 23rd, 1988, Patrik Sundstrom had 8 points in a playoff game against Washington. On April 23rd, 2006, another Patrik, Elias, had 6 points in a playoff game versus the Rangers. Two Patriks, same day, big points. I guess the Jersey

Lecavalier (right) was the first overall pick in the 1998 draft. PHOTO: JIM MCISAAC/THINKSTOCK

Devil, made them do it...No player played for all three teams—Scouts, Rockies and Devils.

QUEBEC NORDIQUES (1979–95): The only first-place team in the NHL to move cities. The Nordiques finished with the best record in the Eastern Conference in the lockout-shortened season of 1994–95. After a quick playoff exit at the hands of the Rangers and the Quebec government hiding their wallets, the financially troubled Northmen were on the move to Denver, where the **COLORADO AVALANCHE** (1995–present) won the Stanley Cup the following spring. Joe Sakic was the last player left on the Avalanche who played for the Nordiques. Colorado has won two cups, in 1996, just after they moved, and in 2001.

HARTFORD WHALERS (1979–97): Gordie Howe scored the 800th goal of his career as a Hartford Whaler and he did it on the day that Simon Gagne was born—February 29, 1980. What a leap year! The goal came against eventual Whaler Mike Liut, then of the St. Louis Blues. A few times during the end of the 1980 season, Hartford had a line, consisting of Gordie Howe, Dave Keon and Bobby Hull, that had a combined age of 131 years old. The Whalers only won one playoff series in the team's history, whereas the **CAROLINA HURRICANES** (1997–present) won a Stanley Cup in 2005. Glen Wesley was the only remaining Whaler on the Hurricanes.

EDMONTON OILERS (1979–present): The only World Hockey Association (WHA) expansion team to win the Stanley Cup, and they did it five times from 1983 to 1990. Out of all the famous players throughout Oilers history, perhaps the most *infamous* is Steve Carlson. This one-time roommate of Wayne Gretzky's played one of the Hanson brothers in the movie *Slap Shot*.

WINNIPEG JETS (1979–96): There were no Stanley Cup appearances for the original Jets, the **PHOENIX COYOTES** (1996–2012), or the **ARIZONA COYOTES** (2012–present). The Jets however won three WHA championships, including the last one. Whereas the

Coyotes have won a total of two playoff series and those both came in 2012. At this writing they haven't won since.

SAN JOSE SHARKS (1991–present): No trips to the Cup Final, yet—but they are trying. Lost in Conference Finals in 2004, 2010 and 2011. At the start of the 2013 lockout-shortened season Patrick Marleau scored two goals in each of the Sharks first four games. First player to do that since Ottawa's Corb Denneny 1917–18. It's been a while. Since 2010, the Sharks are more known for stripping the captaincy from Patrick Marleau and Joe Thornton than winning. I guess they're winning like Charlie Sheen, though.

TAMPA BAY LIGHTNING (1992–present): They've played in five different arenas since their inception. They have seven playoff series wins all-time, and four of them came in the same year: 2004, when they won the Stanley Cup.

FLORIDA PANTHERS (1993–present): Swept by Colorado in 1996 Stanley Cup Final. Missed the playoffs 10 straight seasons between 2001 and 2011. Since their Cup appearance, they've appeared in three playoff series from 1997–2014, winning none of them.

MIGHTY DUCKS OF ANAHEIM (1993–2006); **ANAHEIM DUCKS** (2006–present): Won the Stanley Cup in 2007, beating Ottawa. Almost made the Stanley Cup Final in 2003, only to lose to New Jersey. After winning Stanley Cup in 2007 the team from Anaheim did not make it back to conference finals between 2008–14, despite finishing first in the West once in that span, in 2014. Yes, they were originally called the Mighty Ducks of Anaheim, then the Anaheim Mighty Ducks and then changed again to, simply, the Anaheim Ducks. When you think *mighty*, does a duck ever come to mind?

OTTAWA SENATORS (1993–present): Made it to the Conference Final in 2003, but lost to the Devils in seven games. They were 2007 Stanley Cup Finalists, but then from 2008–14, won only one playoff series. Ottawa has gone 0–4 in playoff series against provincial rival Toronto, between 2000–04.

NASHVILLE PREDATORS (1998–present): Made the playoffs in seven of eight seasons from 2004–12. Never made it to the conference finals. Finally won a playoff series in 2011, against Anaheim. Won another series in 2012, this time against Detroit. Predators have yet to win two series in the same playoff year. The franchise is named for the remains of a sabre-toothed cat found in 1971 during excavation for the construction of a Nashville bank.

ATLANTA THRASHERS (1999–2011); **WINNIPEG JETS** (2011–present): The thrasher is the state bird of Georgia. (Not as fearsome, somehow, as Flames.) The franchise made the playoffs once while in Atlanta, losing to the Rangers in 2007. The Atlanta Flames last playoff series was also a loss to the Rangers, in 1980. Zero playoff series wins for the city of Atlanta, but hey, the Braves won a World Series two seasons after they moved from NL West to NL East. Does it get any more East than Atlanta? Geographically yes, but in baseball, not really.

COLUMBUS BLUE JACKETS (2000–present): Made the playoffs twice, swept by Detroit in 2009 and lost to Penguins in six in 2014. If you're going to lose, might as well do so to a couple of teams that had won the Stanley Cup within the past six years. Daily affirmation. The name Blue Jacket is a reference to the uniforms worn by the Union Army during the American Civil War. That makes two NHL franchise names based on the American Civil War: these Blue Jackets and the Flames, from when Atlanta was burned, upsetting Scarlett O'Hara.

MINNESOTA WILD (2000–present): The Wild have made the playoffs five times. They made the Conference Final in 2003 and were swept by Anaheim. Two of Minnesota's three playoff series wins have come against the Avalanche, whose nickname, coincidentally, doesn't end with an "s" either. The Wild's most interesting story might be when the daughter of Columbus's Jordan Leopold wrote a letter to the Blue Jackets asking that her dad be traded to his hometown team where the rest of the Leopolds were. On March 2, 2015, Leopold was traded to Minnesota. Pass the tissues, I'm getting verklempt.

JERSEY SHORE

IN EUROPEAN FOOTBALL (SOCCER) TEAMS CHANGE THEIR JER-seys all the time. It's a great scheme to make more money, selling more jerseys and other paraphernalia. Money, money, money. NHL teams to an extent have done the same, switching to jersey makers who have their own concepts of what a team's legacy should look like. But that wasn't the case from once upon a time in hockey.

Remember that yellow jersey Team Canada wore in the 2004 World Cup as a tribute to the Winnipeg Falcons that won Olympic Gold in 1920? Of course you do, it was an ugly shirt. If you look at the photo taken after Canada's gold medal win against Sweden in 1920, you'll see that Canada's jersey isn't yellow. It's dark, very dark, perhaps black. But there was an article in a Toronto newspaper during the 1920 Olympics that refers to Canada wearing the yellow jersey in their Olympic game against the United States. Further investigation shows us that the yellow shirt was a practice jersey the team had, and they wore that against the Americans because the U.S. jerseys were dark blue, and, well, black and blue only go together with bruises, not for sporting events. The jerseys Team Canada wore when they won the gold, though, were most definitely not yellow.

The be-leaf (see what I did there?) is that William Hewitt (father of broadcaster Foster), who ran Team Canada, kept the black jerseys as they belonged to the Olympic Committee and the players kept the yellow ones, later adding the Winnipeg Falcons patch to the jersey.

Another factoid about the 1920 Olympic hockey tournament: It was played during the *summer*. The 1920 games were from April until September. Winter Olympics did not begin until 1924, the year that the Toronto Granites won gold for Canada. They wore white, which was fine because it was before Labour Day.

The Canadian flag is red and white but Canada has had various colour schemes over the past 35 years in international competition. When Canada played at the World Men's Championships in 1977 the maple leaf had green and yellow in it. At the 1978 World Junior Championships in Montreal, Canada wore blue jerseys with a white maple leaf. I wonder if that had something to do with the Quebec flag being blue and white? The Team Canada jersey we know today has black in it. Been awhile since Canada had a traditional red and white jersey—you'd have to go back to the 1994 Olympics to find one. My favourite is the red Canada Cup jersey: half maple leaf, with the word *Canada* alongside it. That's class.

3

AT THE DROP OF A HAT

WHERE ELSE SHOULD A CHAPTER ON HAT TRICKS COME BUT chapter number three?

ORIGINS

THERE ARE TWO POSSIBLE SCENARIOS THAT WOULD EXPLAIN the genesis of the term hat trick. (Too bad it's not *three* scenarios—that would make it a hat trick.) The first explanation has its origins in cricket. Yes, there are no goals or nets in cricket, but they do have hat tricks. The term is used when a bowler dismisses a batsman with three consecutive deliveries. My question is this: Would that be a natural hat trick since it was three consecutive, and if the batsmen fouls one off or whiffs at one and gets out on, say, the fourth delivery, is that just a hat trick? Inquiring minds want to know. Cricket has used the term hat trick since the mid to late 1800s. So, technically, they own the term. Scenario two for hockey: Sam Taft owned a men's clothing store in Toronto, and during the 1940s, as a promotional stunt, he would give a hat to any Leafs player that scored three goals in a game. I wonder if the players wore the hats backwards or with the tags hanging off them.

WHICH CAME FIRST?

WHO HAD THE FIRST NHL HAT TRICK? IT WAS A FOUR-WAY TIE.
On opening night in the NHL's existence, in 1917, every team had a player with a hat trick. Joe Malone had five goals for the Canadiens, Cy Denneny popped three for Ottawa, Harry Hyland scored three for the Wanderers and Reg Noble notched four for Toronto. To break it down even further: Malone had five goals before Denneny had three, so he wins the tiebreaker in that game. Harry Hyland had three goals before Noble had two, so chalk that one up to Hyland. So who wins between Hyland and Malone? Unfortunately we can't go to a shootout. Both players' hat trick goals were the second goals of the second period in their respective games. Malone scored his goal with 11:30 remaining in period two. Hyland picked up his hat trick with five minutes remaining in the second period. So, technically, the first NHL hat-trick goes to Malone. The first natural hat trick goes to Hyland. His three goals were all in a row, numbers, three, four and five for the Wanderers. Newsy Lalonde interrupted goals one and two for Malone. Malone did score three in a row for the Canadiens, however goal three came in the third period.

THAT WAS FAST!

THE FASTEST THREE GOALS IN NHL HISTORY SCORED BY ONE
player came off the stick of Hall of Famer Bill Mosienko of the Chicago Blackhawks (spelled Black Hawks then). He wasn't a Hall of Famer at the time, of course, but this accomplishment certainly helped.

On March 23rd, the last day of the regular season in 1952, Mosienko scored three goals in 21 seconds on Lorne Anderson of the New York Rangers. Chicago trailed the Rangers 5–2 at the end of two periods and then New York had a sixth goal to take what would ordinarily be considered a commanding lead. Mosienko then scored three goals at 6:09, 6:20 and 6:30. Gus Bodnar assisted on all three. According to my good buddy Stan Fischler, who was at the game, just after the natural hat trick, Mosienko hit the goal post causing Chicago's head coach Ebbie Goodfellow to say "what, are you in a slump?"

Sid Finney then scored twice for Chicago, including the winner with 38 seconds remaining in the game. Finney had six goals on the season. And if you haven't guessed by his name, yes, Finney was born in Ireland.

Besieged goalie Lorne Anderson never played in the NHL again. That's the opposite of going out on a high note like George Costanza. Five goals in a period—goodbye T-Bone!

It's interesting to note that pictures of Mosienko after the game holding three pucks, show him with the captain's C on his jersey, yet he was never officially the captain of the Black Hawks. Jack Stewart was the Chicago captain that season.

The second fastest three goals were scored by Jean Beliveau. He notched three goals in 44 seconds on November 5, 1955 against the Bruins in Montreal. Beliveau scored the goals in the second period, at 0:42, 1:08 and 1:26. Montreal was trailing 2–0 going into the period; they would win 4–2. Beliveau scored all four goals, Bert Olmstead assisted on all of them.

GORDIE HOWE HAT TRICK

ARGUABLY THE MOST LAUDED UNOFFICIAL STAT IN NHL HISTORY is the so-called "Gordie Howe Hat-Trick," in which a player gets a goal, an assist and has a fight in a single game. It pretty much represents a player "showing up" in all aspects of the night's on-ice activities. For the better part of a half-century nobody questioned the origin of the term; it was naturally assumed that Howe picked up a goal, assist and a fight in a game, once or twice a week. Seemed logical, Howe was, after all, Mr. Hockey, he had no problems picking up points and he was tough as nails—everybody was afraid of him.

Ah yes, everyone was afraid of him. When it was time to go through 26 years of Howe's game logs, I discovered that he had 21 career fights, including playoffs. That's less than one per year, let alone one a week. It would appear that everyone feared a fight with Howe.

So, only 21 fights dramatically reduce the GHHT possibilities for Mr. Hockey. In fact, Howe didn't pick up his first goal-assist-fight combo until the game in which he had his thirteenth career scrap. This occurred on October 11, 1953 in a game against Toronto—he fought Fern Flaman. Howe had one goal and two assists in the game. In three games in which the Saskatchewan native had the GHHT, he had two assists. That adds to the legend, because the real clincher for the stat is getting that one assist. The other games that Howe accomplished the feat were on March 21, 1954, also against Toronto, when he fought Ted Kennedy and had one goal and two assists. Howe's final GHHT occurred in the game where he also had his final career fight—October 26, 1967 against the Oakland Seals. Howe had two goals, two assists and he fought

Gordie Howe scores his 545th goal and passes Maurice Richard as the NHL's all-time leading goal scorer. PHOTO: AP/THE CANADIAN PRESS

Wally Boyer, which makes sense, since he used to play for Toronto. Interesting to note that October 26 is also the date of the shootout at the O.K. Corral (in 1881). Wyatt Earp and Gordie Howe—both legendary enforcers, or were they? That's a story for another time.

The first NHL player to have a goal, an assist and a fight in the same game was Harry Cameron of the Toronto Arena. That was on December 26, 1917. In true Gordie Howe style, Cameron had two assists in the game, to go along with four goals. Cameron fought Billy Coutu. Coutu was kicked out of the NHL ten years later for punching a referee. Why so angry?

If Howe only accomplished the trifecta three times, and he wasn't even the first to do it, why is it named for him? Howe's agent came up with the term. (I guess he was better at marketing than looking at game sheets.) The rights holder should be Cameron, he did it first. It also should be one goal, two assists and a fight. Howe had two assists each time, and Cameron had two when he picked up the first "Gordie Howe" Hat Trick in NHL history. So, we should officially change the unofficial stat of the Gordie Howe Hat Trick (one goal, one assist and a fight) to the Harry Cameron Hat Trick and make it one goal, *two* assists and a fight. It's not a real stat, so we can change it if we want to!

The Gordie Hat Trick used to be a big deal, but in recent years Francois Beauchemin and Kris Versteeg both picked one up. Not to slight those guys, but neither of them are on the fast track to the Hall of Fame. Can you tarnish a legend, when the legend should have never happened to begin with? Is that a riddle?

Howe had 19 real hat tricks in his career. But he never scored more than three goals in a game.

A SPECIAL BIRTHDAY GIFT

Gordie Howe was born on March 31, 1928. How popular was it for a player to have a Gordie Howe Hat Trick on the man's birthday? Not often. Boston's Lyndon Byers had one in 1990 against Montreal—he fought Todd Ewen. There was a 29-year gap until another player had one and it was another Boston player: Zdeno Chara. He accomplished it against Tampa Bay, fighting Evgeny Artyukhin. None after 2009. Sorry Gordie!

A VARIETY OF HATS

THERE ARE A COUPLE OF OTHER NOTABLE VARIATIONS OF THE traditional three-goal hat trick. There's the Mario Lemieux Hat Trick, which is incredible. It came on New Year's Eve 1988 when Mario Lemieux scored five times—one at even strength, one on the power play, one while shorthanded, one on a penalty shot and one into the empty net (with one second remaining). Lemieux did this against New Jersey. Bob Sauve and Chris Terreri were the netminders—for four of the goals anyway. Lemieux had eight points in the game; it was the second time that season he had eight points in a game. Pittsburgh beat New Jersey 8–6, despite the fact that the Penguins only had 19 shots on net.

Wayne Gretzky is the only other player to pick up eight points in a game twice in one season. And one of the games was against New Jersey as well. The Oilers beat the Devils 13–4 on November 19, 1983. Gretzky had a hat trick in the game, while Jari Kurri had five goals, four at even strength and one on the power play. Paul Coffey played on the winning side in both Lemieux's and Gretzky's eight-point games. In 1983 he had a goal and in 1988, an assist. Several Devils played in both games.

Jarome Iginla came close to the Lemieux Hat Trick in a game against Phoenix on February 23, 2003. Iginla fell a penalty shot short of the achievement. Included in those four goals was Iginla's 200th of his career. On the topic of Iginla, he's had five Gordie Howe/Harry Cameron Hat Tricks in his career.

And let's not forget the Bernie Nicholls Hat Trick: a goal in each period, including overtime. It has happened twice. One, of course, by Nicholls. And the other by Sergei Fedorov. Nicholls set the period-by-period bar on November 13, 1984 against Quebec. The Kings won 5–4. The only other player to score for L.A. was

Jarome Iginla won the Art Ross Trophy in 2001–02. PHOTO: RICH LAM/
THINKSTOCK

Phil Sykes. Twelve years later, it was Fedorov's turn. The score was the same, but Fedorov scored all five goals for the Wings as they beat Washington.

Calgary's Theo Fleury is the only player in NHL history to pick up a hat trick wherein all of the goals he scored were shorthanded. It happened on March 9, 1991 against St. Louis. Flames won, 8–4. The first goal came with Al MacInnis in the box; it was assisted by Stephane Matteau and Frank Musil. Guess who was in the box for the other two goals? Matteau for the second and Musil for the third.

Theo Fleury once had three shorthanded goals in a game. PHOTO: AP-RON FREHM/THE CANADIAN PRESS

So you could say that M&M were in on all of the goals. Goal two was assisted by Doug Gilmour and the third was unassisted.

TIME FOR A HAT RACK!

TAKE A GUESS AT WHO HAD THE MOST HAT TRICKS IN NHL history? Wayne Gretzky had 50. Gretzky had 37 three-goal games, nine four-goal games and four five-goal games. Next on the trick list is Mario Lemieux with 40. Mike Bossy right behind him at 39.

Bobby Orr holds the record for most hat tricks in one season by a defenceman. Orr had four three-goal games in 1973–74. But #4 never had a four-goal game in his career. Meanwhile, the most goals scored in a game by a blueliner was five, by Ian Turnbull. No other pointman has accomplished the Turnbull hat trick. Turnbull scored the quintet of lamplighters against Detroit in a 9–1 Toronto win on February 2, 1977. The game was scoreless after the first period. Turnbull had two goals in the second period and three in the third. Turnbull had gone through a span of 30 games without a goal earlier in the season. Several defencemen have had four goals in a game, including Turnbull when he was with the Kings in 1981.

The highest score ever in an international game was 47–0. Canada defeated Denmark by that score on February 12, 1949 at the World Championships. Here were the goal scorers, maybe you're related to one of them?: Jim Russell (8), Tom Russell (6) (not related), Don Stanley (5), Joe Disvastiani (5), Don Munro (5), Ray Bauer (3), Bud Hushey (3), Joe Tergeson (3), Emile Gasine (3), Barney Hillson (3) and Bill Dimock (3). It's interesting that everyone who scored had at least a hat trick. That's 11 hats—13 if you give two each to the Russell boys. Who was in net for Denmark? Apparently nobody.

LORD STANLEY'S HAT

THERE IS A BIT OF DEBATE OVER WHO HAD THE FIRST STANLEY Cup hat trick in NHL history. The NHL began in 1917 and teams from that league squared off against the Pacific Coast League champion for the Stanley Cup until 1926. One publication had the first Stanley Cup hat trick going to Alf Skinner of Toronto against the Vancouver Millionaires in Game Two back in 1918. The box score shows Skinner with two goals, though. All box scores show no one with a three-goal game in the 1918 Cup Final. My research shows that the first hat trick by an NHL player in Stanley Cup history was by Newsy Lalonde of the Montreal Canadiens. It came on March 22, 1919 against Seattle.

A HAT TRICK OF HATRICK BROTHERS

HOW ABOUT THE HATRICK BROTHERS? ED, RAY AND JAMES. THE trio played in the Metropolitan American Hockey League, a league primarily for New York–area players, in the late 1940s. I'm serious—they existed. You can't make this stuff up. Well you could, but that's dishonest and that's how myths are started.

4

WHO ARE THESE GUYS?

REMEMBER WHEN EVERYONE'S FAVOURITE FORMER EXPO Pedro Martinez said, "Who is Karim Garcia?" Or in *Major League* the movie when the grounds crew say "who are these f-ing guys?" That's kind of what this chapter is about—the unsung of the unsung. Except from now on in this chapter I'll just talk about hockey players—promise.

OH BROTHER WHERE ART THOU?

ONE OF MY FAVOURITE TRIVIA QUESTIONS (YES, I SAY THAT A lot—if I didn't have plenty of favourites, we wouldn't have this book, now would we?): What set of brothers have combined for the most points in NHL history? Right away you get guesses of the Stastnys, the Richards, all six Sutters. How about the Gretzkys? Pardon? Wayne and Brent. Remember Brent? He played 13 games with Tampa Bay from 1993 to 1995. Tampa Bay won one of those games. Bad Luck Brent. All told, he had four points with the Lightning. So when you add it to Wayne's 2,857, that gives them 2,861 and ahead of all other brother combinations.

Wayne and Brent faced off against each other once—they literally did faceoff. There is a picture of the two of them taking a draw against each other on October 20, 1993 in Tampa Bay. The Kings won the game 4–3. Wayne had one goal and two assists. Brent had nothing, not even a shot on net.

Some other brother combinations you may not have heard of: Larry Robinson played one game in Montreal with his brother in 1979–80. His name, wait for it, Moe. Larry and Moe. That's right, I'm not making that up. Too bad there was no Curly or Shemp to join them. Moe had no points in his one NHL game. Tough to pick up points when your brother is constantly poking you in the eyes and slapping you in the back of the head.

Mario Lemieux's brother Alain had some success in the NHL, with 119 games played, 24 goals, 48 assists, 72 points. Most of his time was spent in St. Louis and Quebec but he did play one game with the Penguins during Mario's tenure.

Gordie Howe had a younger brother, Vic, who played in the NHL. He played 33 NHL games all with the Rangers in the first half of the 1950s. With only six teams in the NHL in the '50s, the Howes would have met several times. I looked at the game logs, and at least Gordie never got into a fight with Vic. Unclear if Vic got an elbow in the ear from Gordie. Probably, though. Vic had three goals and four assists during his time in the NHL. He was traded to the Rangers along with Andy Bathgate, so that's worth bragging about.

Mark Messier had an older brother named Paul that played briefly with the Colorado Rockies in 1978–79, a year before Mark Messier and the Oilers joined the NHL. Paul had zero points in nine games with Colorado. Here's another great trivia tidbit: Paul was born in England, Mark was born in Edmonton.

Speaking of brothers who played in the NHL that were born in different countries than each other, here are some more: the Reghrs—Robyn (Germany), Richie (Indonesia);. the Folignos— Marcus (United States), Nick (Canada). What's even more interesting about the Folignos is that, in international competition, Nick has played for the United States and Marcus has played for Canada.

How rare is it for hockey brothers to play for different countries? In 1960, at the Squaw Valley Olympic Games, Frantisek Tikal

The Jackson brothers, Art (right) and Harvey "Busher" (left). Art Ross is in the middle. PHOTO: COURTESY OF THE BOSTON PUBLIC LIBRARY, LESLIE JONES COLLECTION

played for the Czechs and his brother Zdenek played for the powerhouse Australians who gave up 88 goals in eight games while scoring just ten. Meanwhile Robert Reichel has always played for the Czech Republic. His brother Martin has represented Germany internationally. One of the perks of playing hockey in Germany is they give you a German passport, making you eligible to play for Germany internationally, providing you haven't played for another country previously.

Teemu Selanne has an identical twin brother. Though, apparently, the Finnish Flash's brother was better at soccer than at hockey.

#99 IN YOUR PROGRAM, #1 IN YOUR HEARTS

THE ICONIC #99 IS KNOWN THE WORLD OVER AS THE NUMBER of Wayne Gretzky, not to mention Ricky "Wild Thing" Vaughn in *Major League* (okay, sorry—had to drop another baseball reference in there). Here's a look at some other #99s in the NHL.

I guess during the Oilers first year in the NHL a couple of other guys thought that 99 was a cool number. Wilf Paiement chose #99 when he was traded to Toronto by the Rockies in 1979. Paiement did the number justice: he had 48 points in 41 games after the trade and then in 1980–81 he had 97 points. Paiement also had 145 penalty minutes that season. All that time in the box—feel shame—stopped him from a 100-point season.

Rick Dudley also wore #99 briefly in Winnipeg. I think Dudley did it as foreshadowing. He picked up five assists in 30 games with Winnipeg, which gave him 99 career assists—and he never played in the NHL again. Way back in the 1930s, the Canadiens had a few players that wore #99 in the 1934–35 season. Joe Lamb, Des Roche and Leo Bourgeault. Lamb had the most success with it; he had five points in seven games.

Four Canadian teams had a #99 on their roster. And three American teams did, because Gretzky played for L.A., St. Louis and the Rangers. See, that's another trick trivia question: name three U.S.–based NHL teams that had a player wear #99. People always look beyond the obvious.

ONE-HIT WONDERS

PERHAPS THE NHL'S MOST FAMOUS ONE-HIT WONDER WAS Don Cherry. Cherry played his lone NHL game with the Bruins against the Canadiens on March 31, 1955, Game Five of their playoff series. The Bruins were down a couple of defencemen due to injury, so the Grape One got the call. Montreal won the game 5–1 and went on to face Detroit in the Stanley Cup Final. Kind of funny when you think about it: Boston was short men for a playoff game in Montreal and Cherry got the call. Twenty-plus years later, Cherry, as coach of the Bruins, becomes infamous for having too many men on the ice in a playoff game in Montreal. It's all connected.

ONE AND DONE

I KNOW WHAT YOU'RE THINKING (BECAUSE I HAVE DIRTY Harry–type instincts). Did any player ever go full Costanza and be a one-hit wonder and go out on a high note? Why yes. A few have…

Rolly Huard was the first player to play in one NHL game and score one goal. Huard was playing for the Toronto Maple Leafs on December 13, 1930 against Boston. The Leafs had injuries to forwards Baldy Cotton and Charlie Conacher. Huard was called up with Hap Hamel. Those two were put on a line with the NHL's first-ever player from Wisconsin, Roger Jenkins. Huard scored the first goal of the game on Cecil "Tiny" Thompson. That was kind of it; Boston won 7–3. Huard should have gone straight to the dressing room after the goal, he hung around too long. He was sent back down to the International League after the game, and went on to score only six goals in that IHL season. Huard played three more seasons in the minors and that was it. Hamel got to play in one more game that season, no points.

Dean Morton also had one game and one goal. Morton made his NHL debut on October 5, 1989 in Calgary as a member of the Detroit Red Wings. It was the season opener for both teams. Morton scored the first goal of the season for the Red Wings. He scored on Mike Vernon. The game was a shootout with the Flames winning 10–7. Morton was sent down to the AHL the next day. Morton changed professions and became an NHL referee a few years later and as of this writing has been doing just fine as an official.

Talk about going out on a high note: Brad Fast scored in the final game of the 2003–04 season. He tallied the tying goal for Carolina in a 6–6 tie with Florida. The goal came with just over two minutes remaining in the third period. Carolina led the game 4–0 at the end of the first period, then Florida scored six straight goals, three in the second period and three in the third period. Fast was off to Switzerland to resume his hockey career the following season, the year of an NHL lockout. In that game Kamil Piros scored his only goal of the season, also in the third period and he never played in the NHL again.

Record of the teams with a one goal, one game wonder: 0–2–1.

A guy that almost fell into this category is Jeremy Williams. In 2005–06 he played one game with Toronto and scored. It was the final game of the season. In 2006–07 he was called up for one game, and he scored again. That game was on February 26. Here you have a guy, two games, two goals. Gold Jerry. You have to keep this guy up. Nope. Sent back to the AHL. In the following season Williams gets called up on February 27, he scores again. Three years, three games, three goals. That's some kind of a hat trick.

ONE-GAME GOALIES

NHL teams once upon a time carried only one goalie on their roster, so when he was injured, teams went looking for help. There were no Jamie McLennans until the 1950s.

"Hey Abbott." As in George Abbott. November 27, 1943 was another Saturday night in Toronto, and the Bruins were in town. Boston's regular netminder, Bert Gardiner had the flu and couldn't play. The Bruins didn't have a back-up goalie. Boston's manager, Art Ross, considered going in net himself. Then he came across the Leafs practice goalie and theology student, George Abbott. I guess it was net at first sight, because Abbott joined the Bruins for the game. It must have felt like Leafs practice all over again because they fired 52 shots at the soon-to-be ordained minister. Abbott gave up seven goals and suffered a concussion, thanks to a Babe Pratt slapshot. Bob Davidson picked up his first NHL hat trick in the game. No word if he bought Abbott dinner afterwards. King Clancy officiated the game.

The most famous one-game NHL goalie has to be hall of famer, Lester Patrick. Patrick who was the manager of the New York Rangers in 1927–28 had to go in net during Game Two of the Stanley Cup Final in Montreal against the Maroons. The Blue Shirts' regular goalie, Lorne Chabot, was injured halfway through the first period, when he took a shot off the left eye from Nels Stewart. Patrick asked the Montreal club if he could use Ottawa goalie Alec Connell as a substitute. Connell was at the game as a spectator. The Montreal players said no, the Rangers had to use a player from their club. With no one else to play net, Patrick put on the pads and went in between the pipes with the score tied at zero. A lifelong defencemen in the Pacific Coast Hockey Association, the 44-year-old was making a heck of an NHL debut. Since Patrick was on the ice, the Rangers had no one behind the bench. So, they borrowed a manager; they grabbed Odie Cleghorn the Pittsburgh Pirates bench boss. The rest of the second period remained scoreless. Less than a minute into the third period, Bill Cook scored for the Rangers. It looked like New York would hold onto the 1–0 lead but Nels Stewart tied the game with just over five minutes left. Into overtime the teams went. Just over seven minutes into the extra session Frank Boucher scored on Maroons goalie, Clint Benedict to give the Rangers the win and even the series 1–1. The next day, New York signed Americans goalie Joe Miller to replace Chabot and Patrick. The Rangers won the Stanley Cup three games to two, becoming just the second American-based team to capture the trophy. This wasn't the first time that Lester Patrick had played in net in a pro-hockey game. Not even the first time against the Maroons. In 1922, Patrick was the manager of the Victoria Cougars of the PCHA. The Cougars were playing the Vancouver Maroons. Cougar's goalie Hec Fowler received a 10-minute misconduct. Patrick, without pads, went in net and didn't give up a goal. The Cougars won the game by one.

THE GUYS FROM HOCKEY'S HOT BEDS

NOW, BY HOT BEDS I DON'T MEAN, ONTARIO, QUEBEC, ETC., where the NHL gets most of its players from. I mean hot as in weather. Here's a look at some players who are from places that are more known for producing warm weather than professional hockey players. Here are some of the players of interest from these balmy locales. (We'll do this ordered alphabetically rather than by humidity.)

ALABAMA has produced two NHL players. Aud Tuten, born in Enterprise on January 14, 1915, played 39 games with the Chicago Black Hawks from 1941 to 1943. He then was out of the game for three years as he fulfilled his duties to the Canadian military. Although born in the Heart of Dixie, Tuten grew up in Western Canada and played his junior hockey in Saskatchewan. Currently hockey is being played at the junior level in Alabama. At the University of Alabama (insert *Forrest Gump* joke here) and at the University of Alabama in Huntsville. Plenty of local talent on both teams. Aud Tuten may have some company in the NHL in a few years. Jared Ross from Huntsville played 13 games with the Flyers from 2008 to 2010. No points. So, Tuten is still leading the way.

ARIZONA'S Jim Brown, not the running back, was born in Phoenix in 1960. Brown spent his youth in the New York area and played junior hockey at Notre Dame. He played three games in the NHL with the Kings. Northern Arizona University has produced one NHL player: Greg Adams, the B.C. native, played two years at NAU and then went on to play over 1,000 NHL games. The Flyers' Sean Couturier was born in Phoenix when his dad played for the Phoenix Roadrunners of the International Hockey League in the early 1990s. The younger Couturier played for Canada at the World Junior Championships in 2011 and was a first-round pick of the Flyers in the same year.

Not only has **AUSTRALIA** produced a professional hockey player, they produced a hall of famer. Tommy Dunderdale was born in Australia in 1887. After living in England, Dunderdale and his family moved to Ottawa, where Dunderdale, at age 17, put on skates for the first time. Dunderdale never played in the NHL; he played in the predecessor NHA and in the NHL's Stanley Cup–rival league, the Pacific Coast Hockey Association. Dunderdale was inducted into the Hockey Hall of Fame in 1974.

There's been two NHL players born in **BRAZIL**. One (goalie Mike Greenlay from Vittonia, Brazil) was raised in Calgary, and the other (Robyn Regehr) played in Calgary. Greenlay played junior at Lake Superior State and for Saskatoon and played just two NHL games, both with Edmonton in 1989. Regehr was born in Recife, Brazil but raised in B.C. The big defencemen played on the Flames blue line. All Brazil needs to do now is to produce a forward.

There have been four players from **FLORIDA** to lace up the skates in the NHL. Three of them played their junior hockey in Canada. Dallas Eakins was born in Dade City (yet was named for a city in Texas). Eakins spent most of his youth in Peterborough where he played minor hockey before joining the Petes. Eakins flourished as a coach for the Toronto Marlies in the American Hockey League... Sticking with Toronto, Val James from Ocala, Florida played briefly with the Maple Leafs. His whole NHL career was brief: 14 games and no points. James grew up on Long Island, New York and then ventured over to the Quebec junior league...Before joining the Oshawa Generals, Leesburg, Florida native Dan Hinote was in the Army, being all that he could be. There was even talk that Hinote was interested in becoming an FBI agent. Maybe he actually is one and undercover in the NHL, playing in St. Louis and Colorado... Blake Geoffrion, the grandson of Montreal legend Bernie "Boom Boom" Geffrion, was born in Plantation. He went through the U.S. Junior system and then to the University of Wisconsin on his way to the NHL. When he pulled on his jersey for the Montreal Canadiens, he became a fourth-generation Hab. His dad Danny played for the Canadiens, as did Boom Boom, of course, and Boom Boom's father-in-law, the great Howie Morenz.

GEORGIA has been represented twice in the NHL. Eric Chouinard, the son of Guy, was born in Atlanta as his parents packed up to move across the continent to Calgary. Eric Chouinard spent less than two weeks in the city where he was born. Chouinard played his junior hockey in Quebec and he played in the 1999 and 2000 World Junior Championships for Canada. Chouinard last played in the NHL in 2005...Mark Mowers was born in Decatur before moving to New York state. Mowers played some minor hockey in Michigan before attending the University of New Hampshire. Mowers played just under 300 NHL games, lastly for the Ducks in 2007...Jean-Marc Pelletier, another Atlanta-born NHLer with a French name that played in the Quebec league, also played at Cornell. Pelletier played briefly in the NHL, seven total games, lastly on leap day in 2004 for Phoenix. He then spent the remainder of his pro-career in Germany.

HAITI: That's right, Haiti. Claude Vilgrain was born in Port-Au-Prince in 1963. His family moved to Montreal when he was a young lad. Vilgrain played for Laval and the University of Moncton before he joined Team Canada at the 1988 Olympics. He had no points in six Olympic games. The 1988 Winter Olympics seemed to be unexpectedly popular for Caribbean countries. You had Vilgrain and the debut of the Jamaican bobsled team. Vilgrain had a short but decent NHL career, accumulating 53 points in 89 games, most of those with New Jersey.

Graeme Townshend grew up in Toronto but was born in Kingston, JAMAICA. Kingston—Don Cherry must love this guy. *And* he played for the Bruins. Townshend scored but three NHL goals, two with Boston and one with the Islanders.

Unfortunately the player from LEBANON is not named Klinger. Beirut's own Ed Hatoum grew up in Ottawa and played in the Ontario Hockey League with Hamilton before joining the Red Wings. Hatoum had a brief NHL career from 1968 to 1971 split between Detroit and Vancouver. He had three NHL goals.

The NFL's Christian Okoye was the "Nigerian Nightmare." Too bad NIGERIA's Rumun Ndur wasn't a goalie—he could have been the Nigerian Netminder. Born in Zaria, Ndur moved to Sarnia, Ontario at a young age and picked up the game of hockey. Ndur was a Sabres draft pick. Ndur scored two NHL goals, one with the Rangers and one with Atlanta. Both teams had claimed him on waivers, almost exactly one year apart. Ndur departed to play hockey in Europe and retired in 2010.

Since the 2004–05 lockout the population of NHL players from the NORTH CAROLINA has gone from zero to two. Jared Boll has played almost 500 NHL games. Ben Smith has played a handful with Chicago. Smith is from Winston-Salem and Boll from Charlotte. Patrick O'Sullivan lived in North Carolina, but was born in Toronto, where he spent most of his youth. He's represented the U.S. internationally and lists his hometown as Winston-Salem.

Tyler Arnason was born in Oklahoma City, OKLAHOMA when his dad Chuck played minor-league hockey in the Sooner State.

Arnason grew up in Winnipeg, though, in the same neighbourhood as the Leafs' Alex Steen...Burr Williams was born in Okemah in the early part of the 1900s. Not much is known about Williams—he played some junior hockey in Minnesota and spent a lot of his career in the minors. Williams did play 19 NHL games in the 1930s, picking up an assist in his first NHL game. Then he was held off the score sheet for the rest of his career...Dan Woodley is another Oklahoma City–born player. I once heard that there were only two things that came from Oklahoma City. Neither was a hockey player. I guess that saying will have to be changed. Woodley played a lot of hockey in B.C., first in Summerland, before he was selected by Kelowna in the WHL draft. Then he played for the Canucks where he picked up two goals in five games in 1987. That was it for his NHL career—five games and out.

Every single player in NHL history that was born in **PARAGUAY** has won rookie of the year. However, Willi Plett was the *only* player born in Paraguay. No other country can boast that 100-percent success rate like Paraguay. Plett grew up in Southern Ontario and didn't play hockey until he was just about a teenager. Plett picked up nearly 2,600 penalty minutes in his career while having six 20-plus-goal seasons.

Holy Ollie, what a goalie. Olaf Kolzig was born in Johannesburg, the capital of **SOUTH AFRICA**, to German parents. At the age of three Kolzig moved to Canada. He lived in Nova Scotia (where his parents still live) and Toronto. During a world junior championships training camp for Canada, Kolzig was filling out his travel documents. A problem arose when it was discovered that his passport number was too long. Reason being: he had a German passport. Kolzig was unaware that he wasn't a Canadian citizen. Kolzig received some nice Team Canada clothing and was sent on his way back to Tri-City of the Western Hockey League. He enjoyed great success in the NHL with Washington winning the Vezina in 1999–2000.

God bless **TEXAS** and their two NHL players. Mike Christie from Big Springs played just over 400 NHL games including some as captain of the Colorado Rockies…Brian Leetch is from Corpus Christi. (That's interesting—the two Texans are a guy named Christie and a guy from Christi. I wonder if they make good cookies.) Future Hall of Famer Brian Leetch played his youth hockey in the New England area.

Born in Caracas, **VENEZUELA**, Rick Chartraw grew up in Southern Ontario. He was a first-overall pick by Montreal in 1974 from the Kitchener Rangers. Chartraw was traded to the Kings for a draft pick that ended up being Claude Lemieux…Don Spring was born in Maracaibo, Venezuela and grew up in Alberta. He played for Canada at the Lake Placid Olympics picking up an assist. Spring played 254 NHL games, all with Winnipeg. He scored one goal.

WHAT'S IN A NICKNAME?

YOU KNOW YOU'VE MADE IT WHEN YOU HAVE A NICKNAME. Tiger, Sea Bass, The Rocket, Fonzie, The Golden Jet, The Great One…Gibby. Should Gibby count? It's just part of my last name. Anyway, back in the early days of the NHL everyone it seemed had a nickname. Maybe the newspaper guys just wanted to type out one name and not two. In today's NHL they basically cut your name in half and add an *s* or an *o* on the end—very creative.

Let's explore some of the standout nicknames shall we? We shall.

One that always makes me chuckle is George Armstrong's nickname: Chief. Armstrong was captain of the Leafs when they won the Stanley Cup in 1967. His name is 67 percent of that of George Armstrong Custer, an infamous U.S. Army officer who, according to legend, was killed by the Cheyenne in June 1876. You fast-forward nearly 100 years and you have a guy with a name that's synonymous with fighting against Native Americans with the nickname "Chief." Is that like calling a fat guy "Slim"?

George Armstrong was the captain of the last Toronto team to win the Stanley Cup. PHOTO: LIBRARY AND ARCHIVES CANADA/CREDIT: LOUIS JAQUES/ WEEKEND MAGAZINE FONDS/E002505690

"Tiny" Thompson's height was listed as anywhere from 5'3" to 5'10". PHOTO: COURTESY OF THE BOSTON PUBLIC LIBRARY, LESLIE JONES COLLECTION

On the subject of nicknames derived from body type: On January 3, 1932 and the same day in 1933, the Boston Bruins and New York Americans played to scoreless draws. That's right, same day, two years in a row, 0–0. Goalies for those games were Roy "Shrimp" Worters for the Americans and Cecil "Tiny" Thompson for the Bruins. That's right, Shrimp vs. Tiny, and there's a shortage of goals. Worters was five-foot-three and Thompson was five-ten. Apparently the nickname came from a youth team he played on; he was the tallest on the team, so they called him Tiny. The Little John affect, I guess.

Ivan Johnson, who played for the Rangers during the 1920s and '30s, had an unusual nickname: "Ching." It came as a result of Johnson's shots hitting the goal posts a lot. Puck hits iron—makes "*ching*" noise. What do they call you if you hit the mesh a lot? Wayne Gretky. Write that down.

Back in the 1930s and 40s, the Bruins had an entire line with a nickname: the "Kraut Line." It consisted of Woody Dumart, Milt Schmidt and Bobby Bauer. Imagine having a nickname like that during World War II. The three of them left the Bruins for a few years during the war and joined the Royal Canadian Air Force. Maybe it was to escape the nickname.

Milt Schmidt, wearing #15, is seen here with Bill Cowley and Jack McGill. Schmidt was part of the Bruins' "Kraut Line." PHOTO: COURTESY OF THE BOSTON PUBLIC LIBRARY, LESLIE JONES COLLECTION

Bernie "Boom Boom" Geoffrion got his nickname from the "boom" when he hit the puck and the "boom" when it missed the net and hit the boards.

PHOTO: LIBRARY AND ARCHIVES CANADA/CREDIT: LOUIS JAQUES/WEEKEND MAGAZINE FONDS/E002505665

We've already mentioned Bernie "Boom Boom" Geoffrion. But what was the origin of the nickname? One boom was the sound you heard when he took his legendary slapshot; the second boom was when the puck missed the net and hit the boards. That's hilarious. Very creative.

Steve Yzerman gave Red Wings teammate Johan Franzen the nickname, "The Mule." Franzen thought it was because he worked hard. No mirrors in the Franzen household sounds like.

5

RULES ARE MEANT TO BE BROKEN

WITHOUT RULES, YOU HAVE ANARCHY. OR A STREET-HOCKEY game. The NHL has always had some interesting rules, and the creativity of teams and players trying to circumvent the rules has always made for a few laughs.

IT'S GETTING DRAFTY IN HERE

ONE OF MY FAVOURITE ATTEMPTED RULE VIOLATIONS INVOLVES Florida GM Mike Keenan and soon-to-be-superstar Alex Ovechkin. To be draft eligible in the NHL, you must turn 18 by September 15 in your draft year. Ovechkin's birthday is September 17, 1985, which made him eligible for the 2004 NHL draft and born a couple of days too late to be eligible in 2003.

The Florida Panthers didn't let the NHL draft rules get in the way of their selecting Ovechkin in 2003. Panthers argued that since there were four leap years in Ovechkin's lifetime, technically he was born on September 13th, thus making him 2003 draft eligible.

Florida tried to select Ovechkin in the second, fifth, seventh and ninth rounds in 2003. The NHL said *nyet* to that. In reality Florida didn't do anything special with the imaginary Ovechkin picks, unless of course you are a big Kamil Kreps fan, then I apologize. Florida actually had the first-overall pick in the 2003

Alex Ovechkin is a five-time winner of the Maurice Richard Trophy for most goals in a season. PHOTO: AP-GERRY BROOME/THE CANADIAN PRESS

draft, but they traded it to the Penguins who took Marc-Andre Fleury.

Instead of focusing on players you can't take, Florida should have had a rethink on dealing their first-overall pick.

In 1979–80 the NHL welcomed four World Hockey Association teams into the fold: the Edmonton Oilers, Winnipeg Jets, Quebec Nordiques and Hartford Whalers. A lot of the players on these teams were signed to the WHA before they were draft eligible in the NHL. There was more money to be made in the WHA than in junior hockey.

It's often forgotten that Wayne Gretzky was never drafted into the NHL. Before he was draft eligible in the NHL he signed in the rival pro league, the WHA, thus making him ineligible for the NHL amateur draft. In 1979, the year the Oilers joined the NHL,

Colorado had the first overall pick and they took Rob Ramage. If the Rockies were that focused on defence, maybe they would have picked Ramage anyway, even if Gretzky were available. Which would have left St. Louis the option of the 18-year-old Gretzky or Perry Turnbull.

Truth be known, the NHL was drafting players at the age of 20 back in 1979 anyway. The WHA was offering contracts two years prior to NHL draft age. Like the original NHL starting out of spite against the NHA, the WHA was signing younger players out of spite toward the NHL. I think this is where the "taking your net and going home" phrase was invented.

The NHL determined that all of the WHA players weren't eligible to win rookie of the year as the WHA was a professional league and besides, you'd be looking at an extra 80 rookie-eligible players, that's a lot of paperwork.

So Gretzky wasn't drafted, he wasn't rookie of the year material, he was shunned by the NHL. He showed them by setting all those NHL records and winning all of those other awards.

Ray Bourque won rookie of the year in 1979–80. The Bruins drafted him eighth overall with a pick they obtained in a trade with the L.A. Kings. Hey, Gretzky played for the Kings.

Fast-forward 10 years: the Calgary Flames' 31-year-old Sergei Makarov wins the Calder Trophy for rookie of the year. Apparently the WHA was considered more of a real league than the Soviet Union's top league where Makarov played for 14 seasons before joining the NHL. Makarov was drafted by Calgary in 1983 and made his NHL debut six years later—a late bloomer? No, he just wasn't allowed to play.

The NHL eventually changed the rookie rules so a player had to be 25 or younger on September 15 in order to be considered a rookie. Let's be honest, it's kind of ridiculous that a 31-year-old wins that award, everyone was well aware of who Makarov was from the Canada Cups and the Olympics.

In 1990–91 Blackhawks goalie Ed Belfour won the Calder Trophy. He just qualified—he was 25 years old at start of season and 26 when it ended.

CAPTAIN, MY CAPTAIN

REMEMBER A FEW YEARS BACK WHEN THE CANUCKS NAMED Roberto Luongo their team captain? But the NHL said, "ummm, no." The league had a long-standing rule that a goalie could not officially be team captain. In the 1930s, goalies were often a popular choice to be named captain. There was a reason for that: delay of game tactic.

A captain's primary job is to discuss nicely with the officials. Let's face it, it's not about leadership on the ice, it's about leading a debate. Teams capitalized on the anyone-can-be-a-captain rule and often named their goalie. So anytime they wanted to argue a call, goalie comes out of the net, seeks out said official and a conversation ensues. Takes up time. Kind of an artificial time out. Players are tired, no time outs, third-base coach gives the goalie the signal to go and argue a call to slow things down a bit.

By the late 1940s, though, the NHL said no more. The on-ice officials must have thought Montreal's Bill Durnan had bad goalie

Frank Brimsek, from Minnesota, was one of the best U.S.-born goalies and the first stand-up goalie. PHOTO: COURTESY OF THE BOSTON PUBLIC LIBRARY, LESLIE JONES COLLECTION

Roberto Luongo took the Canucks to within a win of the Stanley Cup in 2011. PHOTO: DEREK LEUNG/THINKSTOCK PHOTO

breath and they had no interest in speaking to him ever again. So Durnan was out. But then 60 years later, Luongo was in. The Canucks managed to circumvent the NHL rule against goalie captains by naming three "alternate captains." Only catch was he couldn't have the *C* on his jersey. So he had one painted onto his mask instead.. Though I guess he kind of did have a *C* on his jersey anyway—the Canucks have a *C*-shaped whale as their logo.

Luongo being named captain never really made any sense to me—it was technically against the rules. It's like telling your six-year-old he's the man of the house while you are out. An honourary, essentially fake title and there's no increase in allowance or salary.

50 IN 50*

ONE OF THE MOST IMPRESSIVE FEATS OF STRENGTH IN HOCKEY is scoring 50 goals in 50 games. Maurice Richard was the first to do it in 1944–45, when the NHL had 50-game seasons. Then Mike Bossy followed in 1980–81. After 50 goals in 50 games he finished the season with 18 in 29 games, slumping. Gretzky scored 50 in 39 games in 1981–82, good luck beating that record.

There are players who scored 50 goals in 50 games or less that you won't see in any record books. Reason being, NHL "streaking records" (Frank the Tank not included) include teams' games, not players' games. For example in 1993–94 Cam Neely scored 50 goals in his 44th game, but it was game 66 for the Bruins, so it doesn't count.

Jari Kurri, Alexander Mogilny and Mario Lemieux also fall into this category of "that's a shame." Goes to prove that hockey is a team game (even though there is an *m* and an *e* in the word). Kurri's case occurred in 1983–84. He scored 50 in 50, but it was team game 53. Mogilny, in 1992–93, was most impressive, 50 in 46 games, but it was team game 53, same as Kurri.

Lemieux's first of two such seasons was in 1992–93 as well—a lot of "coulda been a contender" that season. He scored 50 in his 48th game, but due to his various injuries, it was in the 72nd game of the Penguins' season. Three years later, Lemieux scored 50 in 50, but it was the 59th Penguin game of the year.

I guess it's a lot easier to track teams' games than various players or placing asterisks here, there and everywhere. An asterisk looks like a spur, and those hurt.

A STAND-UP GUY

IT'S HARD TO BELIEVE THAT, GIVEN THE STYLE OF PLAY THAT goalies use in this day and age, there was a time when if a goalie's pads touched the ice he received a penalty. The modern butterfly style has made the five-hole goal almost extinct. Goalies practically hit the ice when their opponent crosses the centre line. Goals these days have to be top shelf where you keep the Nutella.

In the early years of the NHL's predecessor the National Hockey Assocation, Clint Benedict was nicknamed "Praying Benny" because he went down to the ice a lot, accidentally of course—on purpose would be a rule violation. The NHL eventually changed the rule to allow goalies to make saves on the ice starting in 1917–18. You know how long a game would take if the whistle went every time a goalie was on the ice? I have no idea, but I imagine it would be a lot.

FORWARD THINKING

IN 1928–29 THE GOALIES WERE VERY HAPPY. OF THE 220 GAMES played in the NHL season, 120 resulted in a goalie notching a shutout. There were 14 entirely scoreless games that season. One game between Toronto and Chicago had no goals and no penalties. The main reason for the lack of scoring back in those days was that the forward pass was banned. So, in essence, you were always going backward. For the 1929–30 season, the forward pass was allowed in the NHL. For comparison: George Hainsworth had 22 shutouts in 1928–29 with a 0.92 goals-against average; in 1929–30 he had just four shutouts and his average went up to 2.42. Tiny Thompson's average went up by a full goal and his shutouts dropped by nine. I guess the dead-puck era was over.

"Tiny" Thompson makes a save. Look at the top of the boards—this game took place pre-1940s, before the NHL switched from fencing to Plexiglas.
PHOTO: COURTESY OF THE BOSTON PUBLIC LIBRARY, LESLIE JONES COLLECTION

6

I'M READY FOR MY CLOSE-UP

FROM THE SILVER SCREEN TO THE FLAT SCREEN AND ALL POINTS in between—a look at hockey in the media outside the boundaries of good taste. Wait, that's not it, exactly. How about: here are a few interesting tales about hockey in mainstream media...Ready, and ... *action*.

THE MIRACLE ON ICE

EVERYONE KNOWS ABOUT "THE MIRACLE ON ICE." WHEN George Bailey saved his brother Harry from drowning in *It's a Wonderful Life*? I thought so. Of course I'm referring to the 1980 Winter Olympics in Lake Placid when the United States beat the Soviet Union. There were *two* movies made about one hockey game—you must remember it. The airing of the actual game on ABC had something in common with the movies, besides the score of the game that is. They were all previously recorded. The game was not shown live in the United States, it was in Canada on CTV— so border towns in the U.S. with access to Canadian TV saw it. Al Michaels' legendary call: "Do you believe in miracles? Yes!" was on tape delay. (Did Al Michaels say "*yes*" before Marv Albert started saying it all the time?)

"The Miracle on Ice" 1980 Olympic game between the U.S. and the Soviets was shown on tape delay in the United States but live in Canada. PHOTO: AP/THE CANADIAN PRESS

ABC's coverage of the Olympics in 1980 was in prime time only. Fifty-one and a half hours of coverage that began after the evening news cost $155 million. The USSR vs. USA game had a 5:00 p.m. start time. Sweden and Finland were playing at 8:30 pm. In order for the games to change start times, all four countries had to vote yes to the switch. It was 3–1 against. Guess who voted yes? The Soviets wanted the game at 5:00 p.m. local time because that would make it midnight in Moscow, which was better than 3:30 a.m. in Moscow. The results of the game, though, were not good for Russia, regardless of the time.

"WHO OWN DA CHIEFS?"

LET'S HAVE A LOOK AT SOME OF THE CAST OF *SLAP SHOT* (1977), the greatest sports movie of all-time, and their hockey claims to fame:

First off, current Ducks coach Bruce Boudreau was in the movie. He wasn't on Paul Newman's Charlestown Chiefs however—he played *against* the Chiefs, for Hyannisport. (He wasn't the guy who wet himself though.) Boudreau played for the Johnston Jets of the North American Hockey League, the league on which the film is loosely based.

Dave Hanson, who played Jack Hanson in the movie, played in 33 NHL games. He had a goal and an assist with the Minnesota North Stars.

Jeff Carlson (Hanson), never saw any NHL action but he played in a few WHA games with the Minnesota Fighting Saints picking up an assist.

Steve Carlson (Hanson) had a nice career playing for a few teams in the WHA. He even played on the Edmonton Oilers with Wayne Gretzky in 1978–79. Carlson collected 80 points in 150-plus games before he joined the L.A. Kings for a season in 1979–80 where he had 21 points.

The third Carlson brother, Jack, was supposed to have played Jack in the movie, but he was called up to play in the WHA when the film shoot began.

I can't find any hockey records for Allan Nicholls, aka Johnny Upton, the captain of the Chiefs. However, his grandfather, Riley Hern, is a Hall of Fame goalie. Hern played for the Montreal Wanderers at the turn of the century.

Like the Carlson brothers, Guido Tenesi (who played Billy Charlebois) was a member of the Johnstown Jets. He also played junior hockey with the Oshawa Generals.

Vancouver native Michael Ontkean (Ned Braden) played three seasons at the University of New Hampshire. He averaged nearly a goal a game.

Ron Docken (Yvon Lebrun) was a back-up goalie for the Johnstown Jets who portrayed a Chiefs forward with very little English.

Jerry Houser (Dave "Killer" Carlson) had a part in another hockey movie. He played Les Auge, one of the final cuts of the United States Olympic team, in the original *Miracle on Ice* film from 1981.

Most of the players from the 1975–76 Johnstown Jets were in the movie, but most had uncredited parts.

Chiefs owner Joe McGrath mentions in the movie that Eddie Shore sent him a player down in Omaha in 1948 who was a terrible… um, let's say…*self indulger* (after all this is a family book). The only team around back then was the Omaha Knights of the United States Hockey League. Gordie Howe played for that team in 1946, so we know it wasn't Howe with the problem. He was too pre-mature. Just prior to being sent to Omaha by the Wings, the 18-year-old Howe received a Detroit windbreaker as his signing bonus. Howe requested it. The following season, Howe was up with the Red Wings wearing #17 as Roy Conacher had #9.

COVER BOY

THE FIRST HOCKEY PLAYER TO APPEAR ON THE COVER OF *Sports Illustrated* was Jean Beliveau. Beliveau graced the cover in January of 1956. No jinx though as Beliveau won the Hart Trophy and the Canadiens won the Stanley Cup.

And who was the first hockey player to transcend the sport itself and be featured on the revered cover of *Time* magazine? If you guessed Gordie Howe, Bobby Orr or Wayne Gretzky you may as well just give up. The answer is Lorne Chabot. Yep. Lorne Chabot. The Vezina-winning Chicago goaltender appeared on the February 11, 1935 cover of the magazine.

7

THAT'S QUITE THE...
COINCIDENCE

SOMETIMES COINCIDENCES ARE JUST COINCIDENCES.
Sometimes coincidences raise a Mr. Spock eyebrow. Sometimes
there are shenanigans involved that turn them into a fake coincidence, like conspiracies, or it was set up to look like a coincidence.
Wait. Now *I'm* confused. Let's read on to clear up this mystery.

THE BARILKO TRIANGLE

THE DEATH THAT IS MOST TALKED ABOUT IN NHL HISTORY IS
that of the mysterious Maple Leaf Bill Barilko. Let's set the scene of
Barilko's final game: It was game five of the 1951 Stanley Cup Final
against Montreal in Toronto. Toronto led the series three games
to one. All four games had gone into overtime. Game five was no
different. Tod Sloan tied the game at two with just 32 seconds
remaining. Then Barilko won the game at 2:53 into period four.
Howie Meeker and Harry Watson assisted on the goal. The Leafs
had just two penalties in the game, both by Barilko, who finished
second in the playoffs in penalty minutes.

A few months later, on August 23, 1951, Barilko went on a
fishing trip on James Bay in a plane flown by Dr. Henry Hudson, a
Timmins dentist. Hudson had been a pilot of six years with a clean
record. They were set to return on August 25. But their plane was

nowhere to be found. Fast-forward eleven years: On June 7, 1962, the body of Bill Barilko was found 45 miles north of Cochrane, Ontario. Barilko and Hudson were traveling in a Fairchild 24 float plane. The plane was found in dense bush, partially submerged in water. The skeletal remains of both men were found strapped to their seats, and they were partly burned, which made investigators believe that they died on impact. Investigators also speculated that the plane was weighed down by the amount of fish that the men caught on their trip. There were several coolers in the plane full of the skeletal remains of fish. The search for Barilko in 1951 was the most costly air search in Canadian history with a price tag of $385,000. Barilko's plane was first found by a helicopter pilot named Gary Fields who was on a timber cruising patrol. Fields noticed the wing of the plane sticking out of the bush. Unfortunately Fields neglected to make note of the exact location of the wreck. He returned to his base and contacted the Department of Lands and Forests and they found the plane again. The search party landed their plane about one and a half miles away from the wreckage and they walked through the knee-deep swamp to reach it. There had been a $10,000 reward posted by the Maple Leafs in 1951 for the discovery of Barilko dead or alive, but that expired at the end of the year, so Gary Fields was not able to collect. Two years before Barilko was found, his family erected a tombstone for him in a Timmins cemetery where he was buried a little over a week after he was found. The Maple Leafs did not win another Stanley Cup until the year Barilko was found.

#99—FAMOUS FOR WAYNE GRETZKY, WILF PAIEMENT, RICKY VAUGHN AND RED BALLOONS

WHEN YOU ADD UP WAYNE GRETZKY'S INTERNATIONAL SERVICE with Canada—World Juniors, World Championships, World Cup,

#99 Wayne Gretzky. He wasn't the captain of the Oilers during their first Stanley Cup win. PHOTO: MIKE RIDEWOOD/THE CANADIAN PRESS

Canada Cup and Olympics—you get the amazing sum of 99 points. How fitting.

ALL IN THE FAMILY, PITTSBURGH-STYLE

SPEAKING OF CONSPIRACY—I MEAN COINCIDENCE: AT THE start of the new millennium, Mario Lemieux was considering selling the Pittsburgh Penguins. Then all of a sudden, coming out of the 2004–05 lockout, Pittsburgh got the number-one draft pick which they used to select game changer Sidney Crosby.

But that's not the coincidence—just a lot of luck, nudge, nudge, wink, wink, say no more.

What is interesting about the Sidney-Mario connection is that Sidney's dad, Troy was selected in the same draft as Mario Lemieux. In 1984, Lemieux was taken first overall, and at #240 Troy Crosby was picked by Montreal.

Troy Crosby was a goalie for Verdun in the Quebec Major Junior Hockey League. Lemieux played for Laval in the same league. Sidney also played in the QMJHL with Rimouski. Troy played on the same team as another Lemieux—Claude. Claude and Mario played together for Team Canada at the 1987 Canada Cup, just a week after Sidney Crosby was born.

Troy never played in the NHL—he played one more year of junior after the draft and hung up the pads until little baby Sid was ready for mini-sticks.

Montreal drafted another goalie in 1984, Patrick Roy, in the third round, 51st overall. Roy has the exact same birthday as Mario Lemieux, October 5, 1965—but that's a story for another chapter. Chapter nine, go ahead, have a look—chapter seven isn't going anywhere.

OLYMPIC CONNECTIONS

THE VANCOUVER CANUCKS WERE SUPPOSED TO HAVE WON the Stanley Cup in 2011—based on the patterns of history, at least. Montreal hosted the 1976 Summer Olympics; the Canadiens won the Stanley Cup in 1977. Calgary hosted the 1988 Winter Olympics, the Flames won the Stanley Cup in 1989. I guess Vancouver, host of the 2010 Winter Olympics, didn't realize that host cities are supposed to win the Stanley Cup the following season. You don't lose it in Game Seven on home ice—not part of the equation.

Speaking of Olympics...The 2018 Winter Olympics in Pyeongchang, South Korea will end on February 25. The popular TV series *M*A*S*H* ended on February 28, 1983. The 35th anniversary of a show based in South Korea is celebrated by the end of the Olympics in South Korea. The setting for *M*A*S*H* was in Uijeongbu, 200 kilometres away from Pyeongchang.

THE CURSE AND COINCIDENCES
OF TERRY SAWCHUK

SO WHY HAVEN'T THE LEAFS WON A STANLEY CUP IN 45 YEARS and counting? Lack of talent? Don't be ridiculous, that makes no sense whatsoever. There have been forces of nature at work that have the Leafs without silverware since before a man first walked on the moon. That man, of course, was Neil Armstrong. The man who captained Toronto's last Cup win? George Armstrong. Coincidence? I think not.

When the Leafs won the Cup in 1967 Terry Sawchuk came off the bench in Game 4 to replace an injured Johnny Bower, who suffered a groin injury. The Leafs lost Game 4 by a score of 6–2 and Toronto fans weren't very happy. In Game Six, in which the Leafs won at home 3–1, Sawchuk was booed by Leafs fans and taunted with sarcastic applause when he made a save. According to the Habs players, Sawchuk *won* the series for the Leafs. Here's a quote from Canadiens goalie Gump Worsley after Game Six: "Sawchuk saved them again, but how about those Leafs fans, eh? Aren't they something? He puts the team in the finals and they boo him because he lets in a couple of soft goals earlier in the series. They weren't always like that around here. It makes you wonder sometimes."

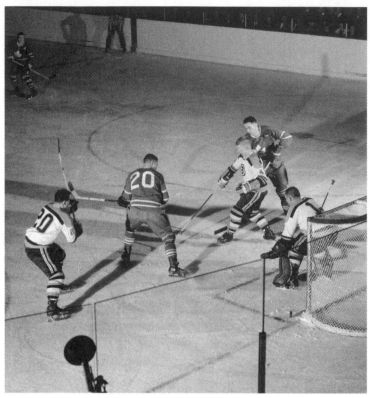

#4 Bobby Orr and Leafs captain George Armstrong battle for the puck.
PHOTO: CITY OF TORONTO ARCHIVES, FONDS 1257, SERIES 1057, ITEM 7527

Sawchuk was 37 at the time of the Leafs Cup win. He had spent 13 of his first 15 NHL seasons in Detroit, and the Manitoba native had asked Toronto to trade him back to the Motor City where his family was living. Instead of obliging the veteran, the Leafs left him unprotected in the expansion draft and he was claimed by L.A. At the time, L.A. was the farthest NHL city from Detroit. Not exactly a good fit for Sawchuk.

The week following Sawchuk's departure from Toronto, the Leafs presented him with the J.P. Bickell Memorial Award. It was given to the player or member of the organization who performed at a high level of excellence over the year or a career. It is not given out every year. In fact since Sawchuk won the award, the only active players to receive the award, have been: Tim Horton (1969), Mike Palmateer (1979), Doug Gilmour (1993) and Mats Sundin/Curtis Joseph (1999).

The closest the Leafs have gotten to the Stanley Cup Final, since the days of Sawchuk, was in 1993, when they led their Conference Final series 3–2 against the L.A. Kings. In Game Six in L.A., Wayne Gretzky had the infamous high stick on Gilmour. Referee Kerry Fraser missed the infraction, which would have seen #99 receive five and a game. Instead, Gretzky played on and scored the winner in OT. The Kings then won Game Seven in Toronto.

What does all of this have to do with the curse of Terry Sawchuk? Sawchuk died on May 31 (1970). Fraser was born on May 30 (1952). Gretzky's high stick was on May 27. Game Seven was on May 29. Forget the Ides of March. How about the end of May for the blue and white? The Leafs are 7–1 all-time at home in Game Sevens in club history. With the loss to the Kings being the only Game Seven at home past the 15th of May.

What team did the Leafs trade Sawchuk to? Oh that's right—the Kings.

Sawchuk wore #30 when the Leafs won the Cup in '67. Seventeen goalies have worn #30 since. Guess how many have won a playoff series? Only Wayne Thomas—one series in 1977.

So has the Late Terry Sawchuk cursed the Leafs? Like the Bambino did the Red Sox? Well of course he has. No other way to explain it. Inferior talent makes no sense.

THE CURSE OF...HAROLD BALLARD?

THEN THERE IS THAT OWNER GUY—HAROLD BALLARD. HE DIED in April of 1990, which is a fitting way to end the regular season— and the Leafs, of course, missed the playoffs. Ballard really is a story for another time. But, what the heck, here's a quick one anyway.

Ballard is the first manager of a Canadian international hockey team to lose a game. In 1933 Canada lost for the first time in international competition when they dropped a 2–1 decision to the United States at the World Championships in Prague. The Canadian team was actually late leaving for the World Championships—Ballard had a financial issue with the organizers. Shocker. This didn't impact Canada's game against the U.S., but it set the groundwork for Ballard's frugalness and non-winning ways with the other Maple Leafs. The losing tradition continued in Toronto: Leafs won only eight playoff series in the almost 30 years Ballard was the boss.

THE VANCOUVER HEX

SOMEBODY ON TWITTER MENTIONED TO ME THAT EVERYTHING bad always happens to Vancouver. At first I just thought it was a fan overreacting—as we all know, everything bad that happens

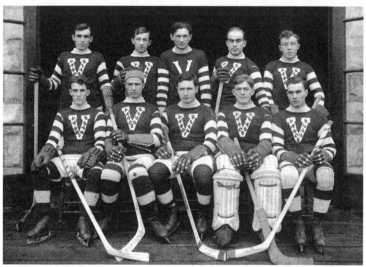

The Vancouver Millionaires won the Stanley Cup in 1915. PHOTO: CITY OF VANCOUVER ARCHIVES, 99-126

in the NHL is against the Leafs. I mean who else blows two 5–0 third period leads? Who does that? Toronto does, against Calgary and St. Louis. But, for argument's sake, let's look at Vancouver. (For the record, I wouldn't call these coincidences, more like interesting observations, because I'm making a Rocky Mountain out of a molehill.)

Errol Flynn died on October 14, 1959 in Vancouver. (Bear with me, here.) The swashbuckling matinee idol was trying to sell his yacht in Vancouver when he suffered a heart attack. Wayne Gretzky's first NHL goal was on Glen Hanlon of the Canucks, on the 20th anniversary of Errol Flynn's death. Meanwhile, another Oiler, Ryan Nugent-Hopkins, notched his first career hat trick against Vancouver, on October 15, 2011, missing the Flynn/Flynn anniversary by just one day.

COLD WITH A CHANCE OF FLEURYS

SOMETIMES PLAYERS THRIVE AGAINST CERTAIN TEAMS, OR IN baseball against certain pitchers, in specific ballparks. In football, Peyton Manning always beats the Texans. It would be considered quite odd that a player would perform well on the same day every year. And it isn't his birthday. Take Marc-Andre Fleury, for instance. He takes it up a notch on March 25. On March 25 in the years 2007, 2008, 2009 and 2011, he had a shutout. On 2012, on the same day, he allowed two goals, but got the win. He was 5–0–0 in his career on the 25th of March with four shutouts. The streak ended in 2014 when Fleury lost to the Coyotes, surrendering five goals That's impressive. Teams he beat: 2007—Boston, 29 saves; 2008—New Jersey, 31 saves; 2009—Calgary, 31 saves; 2012—New Jersey, 21 saves (it was a shootout win). In 2012, third time was the charm for New Jersey—they finally scored on Fleury, but he got the win—34 shots, 32 saves. He tallied a .986 save percentage in the five games on March 25. If you're Marc-Andre Fleury, wouldn't you get one of those page-a-day calendars and leave in on March 25 in your locker? Goalies aren't superstitious, are they?

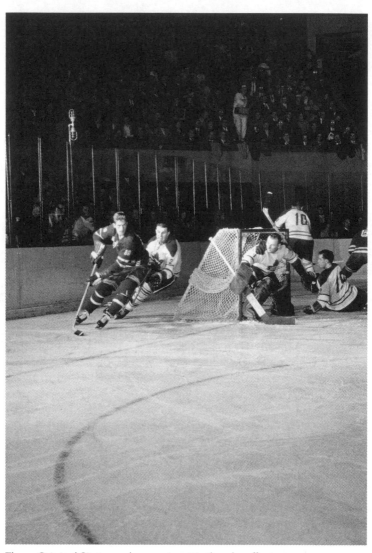

These Original Six teams have not met in the playoffs since 1971. PHOTO: LIBRARY AND ARCHIVES CANADA/CREDIT: LOUIS JAQUES/WEEKEND MAGAZINE FONDS/E002505706

HAPPY BIRTHDAY!

PHIL ESPOSITO WAS BORN ON FEBRUARY 20, 1942 IN SAULT Ste Marie, Ontario. In 1971, 1972 and 1974 he scored his 50th goal of the season on his birthday. In 1971 he became the fourth player in NHL history to score 50 goals. The following two times he upped the ante: In 1972 he scored twice on his birthday to get to 50, and in 1974, he picked up a birthday hat trick. I wonder if he blew out the candles on his cake before the games, making his wish that he'd score number 50?

8

IF YOU AIN'T FIRST, YOU'RE LAST

THERE'S ALWAYS BEEN SOME QUESTION OVER WHO SAID "IF you ain't first, you're last." Ricky Bobby thought his dad Reece said it, Reece denied it. Regardless, they're words of wisdom.

Here are a few notable lasts in hockey history. We'll start with my favourite: I was the last born to Bill and Helen Gibson. Oh. See what I did there? Did a head fake with a stat in order to mention my parents in the book. Thus keeping me in their good books. That's example to follow for anyone—write that down.

YESTERYEAR…OR, YESTERCENTURY, I GUESS

THE LAST PLAYER BORN IN THE 1800S TO PLAY IN THE NHL WAS Ivan "Ching" Johnson (see also page 62), born in Winnipeg on December 7, 1898. Let's connect Ivan Johnson to Sidney Crosby, playing the six degrees of separation game—we'll call it Six Degrees of Sidney Crosby.

Johnson played in the NHL from 1926 to 1938, all in New York, with the Rangers and the Americans. Johnson played with Hap Day in 1937–38 with the Americans; Day played with Turk Broda in Toronto; Broda played on the Leafs with Tim Horton in 1951–52; Horton played with Jim Rutherford in Pittsburgh in 1971–72; Rutherford and Murray Craven were Red Wings in 1982–83;

Craven and Mark Recchi were both in Philadelphia in 1991–92; and Recchi played in Pittsburgh with Crosby. Okay, Seven Degrees of Sidney Crosby.

A NOT-SO-LASTING IMPRESSION

DAVE REECE APPEARED IN 14 NHL GAMES WITH THE BRUINS IN 1975–76, while Boston tried to get their star first-string netminder Gerry Cheevers back from the WHA. On February 7, 1976, with Cheevers watching, Reece had a big problem in Toronto with Darryl Sittler. To the tune of 10 points—6 goals and 4 assists.

Reece, a native of Troy, New York, never played in the NHL again after that game. However he did play for the United States at the 1977 World Championships when Canada and their NHLers made their return to international competition. Sittler did not play in the Worlds until 1982, so no rematch. Reece did not face the red and white maple leafs at the tournament. Mike Curran was in net for that game. Curran played in the WHA and with the NHL's North Stars, which had two of the three "Hanson Brothers" on the team, along with Bruce Boudreau. Where was I? Oh yes, Reece and the Leafs. The Toronto Maple Leafs were eliminated from the NHL playoffs the day Canada beat the U.S. 4–1 at the World Championships, so Reece would have been okay if he did play at the Worlds, no threat of Sittler flying over to play in the game.

THE LAST OF THE BARE HEADS

THE LAST NHL GOALIE TO PLAY WITHOUT A MASK WAS ANDY Brown. The last player to play without a helmet, meanwhile, was Craig MacTavish. You know what they have in common besides lack of head protection? Well, they almost have a Wayne Gretzky connection. Brown was played for the WHA's Indianapolis Racers a full season removed before Gretzky did, and MacTavish, of course, played with Gretzky in Edmonton and St. Louis.

Brown left the NHL in 1974 for the WHA, where he continued to not wear a mask. Brown wore one in practice—nothing worse than getting hurt by a teammate. Brown's father Adam played with Gordie Howe in Detroit. Howe played against Andy in the WHA.

MacTavish's career ended in 1997. He played almost 1,100 career NHL games. He had six straight 80-game seasons, so he must have had a helmet under his hair or something. How else could he have been that durable?

AND THE LAST OF THE LASTS

THE LAST ACTIVE PLAYER FROM THE SO-CALLED ORIGINAL SIX era was Boston Bruin Wayne Cashman, who last played during the 1983 Stanley Cup Playoffs. In his final game, Cashman assisted on a goal by Brad Palmer. Palmer never scored or played in another NHL game.

The last active goalie from the Original Six era was Rogie Vachon, who retired in 1982 with Boston.

Player-coaches were once quite popular. They arguably reached their peak of popularity with Reggie Dunlop, Paul Newman's character in *Slap Shot*. The last player-coach in the NHL existed a good seven years before *Slap Shot* hit the theatres. It was Charlie Burns of the Minnesota North Stars. It's worth noting that Dunlop and his Chiefs ended up in Minnesota at the end of *Slap Shot*.

Okay, speaking of lasts: that's my last reference to *Slap Shot*.

9

BETWEEN THE PIPES

HERE'S A LOOK AT THE MORE INTERESTING STATS, FACTS AND stories from the world of goaltending. Who was that masked man?

THE SIEVES

THERE'S ALWAYS THE DEBATE OVER WHO IS THE BEST GOALIE of all time. Terry Sawchuk, Patrick Roy, Ken Dryden, Martin Brodeur or Denis Lemieux? Tough call. But how about the question of who's the *worst* goalie of all time? Frank Brophy of the 1919–20 Quebec Bulldogs had a goals-against average of 7.11—inspired a convenience store maybe, but not his teammates. The 7.11 is the worst goals-against average in NHL history. Brophy only won three of 21 games in his career.

Don Cherry, meanwhile, would have us believe that Hardy Astrom is the worst goalie. Astrom was signed by the Rangers GM, John Ferguson during the 1977 World Championships. Astrom played four games of mediocrity with New York, not showing off and not falling behind before he was dealt a season later to the Cherry's Rockies where he played below mediocre. Astrom had a stellar NHL debut: he made 29 saves against Montreal at the Forum ending the Habs 28-game unbeaten streak. Astrom was not as horrible as Don Cherry would have you believe. Then again, I've never heard of too many goalies that tried to fake an injury during warm-up so they wouldn't have to play.

As for other candidates for "worst," the record of Washington Capitals goalie Michel Belhumeur speaks for itself. The Sorel, Quebec native played in 42 games with Washington between 1974 and 1976—he had zero wins, 29 losses and 3 ties. Not everything was bad for Belhumeur. He stopped two penalty shots in the same game against Chicago—Jim Pappin and Stan Mikita were the shooters. In his rookie season with the Flyers he won nine games. But part of the problem seemed to always be that Belhumeur got very little support from his teammates over his career. In one of his first-ever starts, Philly played Minnesota and the North Stars fired 32 shots at him in the first period. Things just never seemed to get better for Belhumeur. In one of his last starts in his career with Washington, the Penguins fired 66 shots towards Belhumeur in a 12–1 Pittsburgh win. Not sure if Belhumeur decided to go into hiding after 1976, but no wins in 42 straight games is a record, which will probably never be broken.

GOAL-SCORING GOALIES

NOW ONTO SOME GOALIES WHO WERE GOOD WITH THE STICK. The first goalie to score a goal, in junior or in the NHL, by actually shooting the puck was Chris Clifford of the Kingston Canadians in the Ontario Hockey League. On January 7, 1986 in a game against the Toronto Marlboros, the Canadians led 4–3 late in the third period. Toronto then pulled their goalie Sean Burke. The Marlies had a shot on net, Clifford gloved the puck, skated to the right faceoff circle and shot the puck down the length of ice and into the net. That was a very good year for Clifford, actually. He had eight points. He played a total of 24 minutes in the NHL, all with Chicago, and he never gave up a goal. Not bad to retire with an OHL goal and having never been scored on in the NHL.

There have been ten NHL goalies to light the lamp at the opposite end of the ice in the regular season. Here they are: On November 28,

1979 the Islanders' **BILLY SMITH** scored against the Rockies in Denver. A delayed penalty was called against the Islanders' Mike Kaszycki, so Rockies coach Don Cherry pulled goalie Bill McKenzie for the extra attacker. Colorado had a shot on net and Smith made a chest save and knocked the puck in the corner. Colorado rookie Rob Ramage skated after the puck and blindly shot it back to the point, nobody was there. The puck went into the Colorado net. Originally the goal was given to Dave Lewis, but after video review, Smith was awarded the goal. Billy Smith didn't even start the game—Chico Resch did but he was pulled after some less than stellar play. The Smith goal tied the game at four in the third period. However, Colorado's Gilbert Delorme scored on the power play during the Kaszycki penalty. Colorado won the game 7–4.

The Rockies number one goalie the season earlier was **MICHEL PLASSE**. Plasse scored a goal as well, in 1971, playing for the Kansas City Blues of the Central Hockey League. He scored against the Oklahoma City Blazers. On that Oklahoma team was Dick Cherry, the brother of Don.

Let's recap. First goal by a netminder in junior hockey happened in Kingston, by a Kingston goalie. Don Cherry is from Kingston. First goal by an NHL goalie, happened against Don Cherry's team. First goal by a minor league goalie, happened against Don Cherry's brother's team. (Maybe I should have put all of this in the coincidence chapter.)

On December 8, 1987 Philadelphia's **RON HEXTALL** scored a goal against Boston. It was noted at the time that it took 40,219 games for an NHL goalie to shoot and score a goal. I wonder what the over/under was. With Boston goalie Reggie Lemelin on the bench in the final two minutes, Hextall launched a high shot over all of the Bruins and into the yawning cage to give the Flyers a 5–2 lead, the game's final score. Philadelphia scored four unanswered goals in the third period for a nice comeback win. It was almost déjà vu for Hextall on April 9, 1989. It was during a playoff series against the Washington Capitals. The Caps dumped the puck into the Flyers end, Hextall retrieved it and fired it high down the ice and into the empty net. Hextall's goal capped another four-goal third period for Philadelphia as they came from behind to beat Washington 8–5. Pete Peeters was the goalie for the Capitals in the game.

MARTIN BRODEUR has scored three times. The first came on April 17th, 1997 against Montreal, the second on February 15, 2000 against Philadelphia. Like Hextall, Brodeur has a playoff goal and a regular-season tally. Brodeur's goal against Montreal was in Game One of the series. The Canadiens scored two shorthanded goals in the game but it was Brodeur's Devils that triumphed 5–2 in Montreal. Jocelyn Thibault was on the bench when Brodeur scored. (Side note: Thibault was the last goalie to win at the Forum in Montreal and at Maple Leaf Gardens.) Against the Flyers in 2000, Brodeur picked up the winning goal when the Flyers inadvertently put the puck into their own net during a delayed penalty. Brian Boucher was on the bench. Brodeur had the third goal of the game, Devils won 4–2.

Brodeur also had a first period power-play goal on March 21, 2013 against Carolina. Brodeur knocked the puck into the corner boards in his own end, a delayed penalty call was coming against the Devils. Jordan Staal of Carolina attempted to pass the puck back to the point, it went off the boards past the Hurricanes defencemen and into the net that Dan Ellis had vacated for the extra attacker.

On January 2, 1999, in a game against the Senators, Brodeur had a chance to see another goalie score. Well, sort of. During a delayed penalty call, New Jersey's Lyle Odelein shot the puck past a few teammates and into his own empty net. **DAMIAN RHODES** was credited with the goal. Ottawa thumped New Jersey 6–0. The Rhodes goal came in the first period, which makes him the only goalie to score in a period other than the third. Brodeur was the goalie of record for the Devils in the game.

Two years to the day that Rhodes scored, Montreal's **JOSE THEODORE** scored *and* picked up the shutout. (Happy New Year to Theodore and Rhodes.) Theodore sent a 50-metre back-hander down the ice and into the yawning Islanders cage to seal a 3–0 Montreal win. John Vanbiesbrouck was the Islander goalie in the game.

CHRIS OSGOOD scored against Hartford on March 6, 1996. Sean Burke was on the bench. Detroit won 4–2.

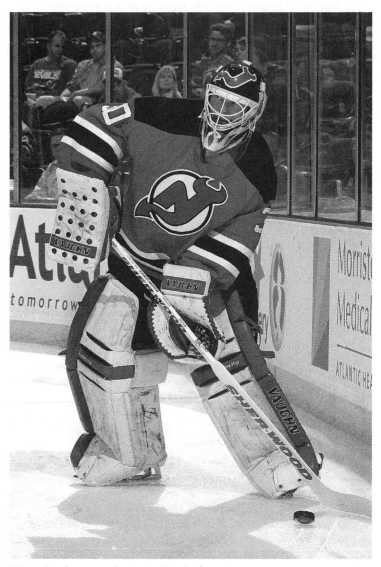

Martin Brodeur won the Vezina Trophy four times. PHOTO: JIM MCISAAC/
THINKSTOCK

EVGENI NABOKOV is the first European-born NHL netminder to score in the NHL. He got his goal on March 10, 2002 at Vancouver. Peter Skudra had taken over in the Vancouver net for Dan Cloutier who was pulled for not stopping the puck on a consistent basis. The Sharks beat the Canucks 7–4.

Buffalo's **MIKA NORONEN** was the next goalie to score after Nabokov. Back to back Europeans. Noronen scored against Toronto on February 14, 2004. It came with 43 seconds remaining in the game and gave the Sabres a 6–4 win,. Noronen was named third star of the game, obviously for scoring the goal, because he, himself, allowed four. Though his goal was actually the result of the Leafs scoring on their own net.

Nashville's **CHRIS MASON** didn't score in the final minute on an empty net, which is generally the custom for goalie goals it would seem. Mason's goal on April 15, 2006 against Phoenix came halfway through the third period. What's up with stat? The Coyotes pulled their goalie for the extra attacker on a delayed penalty and Phoenix scored on their own net and Mason was credited. Mason's goal made it 5–1 for Nashville and that's the way the game ended.

CAM WARD received credit for a goal on December 26th, 2011 thanks to Ilya Kovalchuk. In the final minute of a 3–2 Hurricanes lead, Kovalchuk tried to pass the puck back to the point in the Hurricanes end. Didn't work out so well, down the ice and into the empty net. Ward didn't even get credit for a shot on net.

MIKE SMITH had a beauty goal against Detroit on October 19, 2013. The game was at the Coyotes. With Phoenix (now called Arizona) up 4–2 late in the third period, Mikael Samuelsson of the Red Wings put a shot on net from the blue line. Smith snagged it low with his glove, immediately dropped it in the crease and fired it down the ice. The puck made it across the line with one second remaining. With that kind of hand-eye-stick coordination by Smith, he could be on *Game of Thrones*.

All of the netminders goals were unassisted. Speaking of assists… Here are the top ten leaders in career assist by goalies:

1. Tom Barrasso—48
2. Grant Fuhr—46
3. Patrick Roy—45
4. Martin Brodeur—45 (but he has Roy on goals)
5. Mike Vernon—39
6. John Vanbiesbrouck—35
7. Ed Belfour—34
8. Ron Hextall—32
9. Curtis Joseph—31
10. Sean Burke—28
    (*Includes games played in the 2014–15 season.*)

Grant Fuhr holds the record for assists in one season by a goalie. He got 14 in 1983–84. No goalie has picked up a goal and an assist in the same game. The most points in one game by a goalie is three: Jeff Reese picked up the three assists in a 13–1 Calgary butt-kicking over the Sharks. It was the Sharks' sixteenth straight loss. Ronnie Stern and Robert Reichel had hat tricks for Calgary, Stern also had a fight, but no assists, so he missed out on the Harry Cameron Hat Trick. Reichel had six points in the game. Reese picked up two assists on Reichel goals and one on a Gary Roberts lamplighter. There was one positive for the Sharks in the game: they picked up the only power-play goal. It was the first goal of the game.

MORE THAN ONE USE FOR A GOALIE STICK

IT'S INTERESTING TO NOTE THAT THERE IS NO OFFICIAL RECORD for goalies in the penalty-minute department. Unofficially, Ron Hextall holds the single-season penalty minutes record for a netminder with 113—he did that in 1988–89. It was the third straight season he had over 100 minutes in penalties. He was the only goalie ever to have more than 100 penalty minutes in a season. He also had 584 penalty minutes in his career—the only goalie over 500 carrer minutes. Billy Smith is closest to Hextall at 489.

Ron Hextall was the first NHL goalie to shoot and score a goal. PHOTO: AP-TOM PIDGEON/THE CANADIAN PRESS

One interesting story about Hextall comes from Team Canada's training camp in 1987. Just months after Hextall picked up an eight-game suspension for his stick work on Edmonton's Kent Nilsson, Hextall accidently broke the arm of Sylvain Turgeon during training camp for the Canada Cup. The puck was between Hextall's legs and Turgeon went for the puck, tripping Hextall in the process. As Hextall's feet came out from under him, his stick crashed down on Turgeon's arm breaking it. By all accounts it was an accident—even Turgeon said so. Since Hextall was involved, a lot was made of the incident in the media. Some guys just can't catch a break, while others have it thrust upon them.

THE UNBREAKABLE EDDIE JOHNSTON

EDDIE JOHNSTON HAD AN INCREDIBLE RUN IN 1963–64. HE played in all 70 games for Boston, and outside of getting pulled for an extra attacker—which didn't happen that often—Johnston was in net for pretty much all of the 4,200 possible minutes that season. Johnston took over for Bob Perreault in 1962–63 in a game against Toronto. Then on January 30, 1965 in Toronto, Johnston's streak of 161 consecutive games played came to an end. Johnston had the flu and wasn't supposed to play against Toronto. However, back-up goalie Jack Norris, who flew in from the Bruins minor league affiliate in L.A., had his equipment stolen at a Toronto hotel. So Johnston was forced to play with the flu. Five minutes into the game Johnston took a whack on the hand and it was broken. Johnston finished the game. Boston lost 6–1. The next night in Boston, Norris played in net for the Bruins, wearing Johnston's skates and equipment. Although Johnston's games streak came to an end, his equipment carried on for one more day. Norris lost his NHL debut, 4–2. During his streak, Johnston—who played without a mask—used to occassionally put leeches under his eyes when off-ice to decrease the swelling. He used this tactic often when he suffered a broken nose.

Corey Crawford won the William M. Jennings Trophy in 2012-13 on his way to winning the Stanley Cup with Chicago. PHOTO: BRUCE BENNETT/ THINKSTOCK

THE MASK MAKES THE MAN

SENATORS' GOALIE ANDREW HAMMOND BEGAN HIS NHL CA- reer in 2014–15 with an incredible run of 14–0–1, one shy of the NHL record, 14–0–2, set by Pittsburgh's Patrick Lalime in 1996–97.

Lalime went on to stardom with the Senators in the early 2000s. Not only do Lalime and Hammond share the Senators connection, they also have odd cartoon characters on their masks—Lalime with Marvin the Martian and Hammond with the Hamburglar. Hammond's character is there, obviously, as a play on words with his last name. Lalime, meanwhile, felt that Marvin bears a resemblance to the Senators logo.

10

HODGEPODGE

WITH ALL DUE RESPECT TO HOCKEY BROADCASTING LEGEND
Dave Hodge, "Hodgepodge," in this case, is a reference to the
catchall category in *Jeopardy!* So, don't call this chapter a dumping
ground for miscellaneous trivia that I couldn't shoehorn into any
of the other chapters—because it's totally not...With that in mind,
I'll take "Hodgepodge" for 200, Alex.

DON'T BE SO BOSSY—SIMMER DOWN!

I'M SURE MOST HOCKEY FANS OVER A CERTAIN AGE WILL RE-
member Mike Bossy scoring two goals against the Nordiques on
January 24, 1981 to score 50 goals in 50 games. Bossy did it in
dramatic fashion, scoring twice in the final 4:10 of the game on
Quebec goalie Ron Grahame. (Not to get too sidetracked, but
we can do that in this chapter. Let's be hodgeypodgey: Grahame
didn't play again after that season. His son, John, is also a former
NHL goalie and his wife, Charlotte, worked for the Avalanche as
an office administrator. What do Charlotte and John have in common—aside from the whole mother-and-son thing? They both
have their names on the Stanley Cup. Charlotte with Colorado in
2001 and John with the Lightning in 2004.) Okay, back to Mike
Bossy—so we can move on to Charlie Simmer. On the same

day that Bossy scored two in the third period to get 50 in 50, just over 200 miles away in Boston, L.A. Kings forward Charlie Simmer also scored two goals in the third period, to give him 49 goals in 50 games. Simmer also scored in the second period of that game, his third goal came at 19:59 of the 3rd period, so he had zero chance of scoring 50 in 50. But he would score his 50th in his *next* game, two days later (on Wayne Gretzky's 20th birthday) against the Nordiques. Bad few days for Quebec. Ron Grahame wasn't in net for Simmer's 50th, it was an empty netter, just like Simmer's 49th.

The 1980–81 season was also a breakout year for another player, one not named Bossy or Simmer. Nordiques forward Jacques Richard had 52 goals and 51 assists that season. His highest goal output prior to that season was 27 and 43 points. Talk about taking it up a notch. Richard played two more NHL seasons after that, and the best he did was 15 goals and 26 assists. What happened?

LOCKED OUT

IN JANUARY 2013, THE NHL ENDED THEIR FOURTH WORK STOP-page in league history. Three lockouts and a strike. Although the strike didn't cost any games. It was more of a 10-day break in April 1992—a pretty weak April Fool's joke.

In the NHL's three lockouts, a total of 2,208 games were cancelled. In the NBA, NFL, and MLB combined a total of 2,534 games were cancelled due to work stoppages. Luckily for the NHL they have a ten-year deal in place now so they won't be able to lap the field any time soon.

Who was around for all of the work stoppages? Jaromir Jagr, Martin Brodeur and Gary Bettman. I think in *Glengarry Glen Ross* that qualifies them for a set of steak knives. You may think that's an obscure reference, but the movie came out in 1992, so it is relevant to the strike.

Ten players have been around for all three lockouts: Jagr, Brodeur, Roman Hamrlik, Teemu Selanne, Chris Pronger, Nikolai

Khabibulin, Jason Arnott, Ray Whitney, Sergei Gonchar and Brian Rolston.

The biggest loser financially in the 2012–13 lockout was Ilya Kovalchuk. He was due to make $11 million in salary. Cut the season from 82 games to 48 and you lose $5 million.

Now who could possibly help out Kovalchuk? Shea Weber received a 2012–13 signing bonus of $13 million. All signing bonuses were guaranteed payments. Nice work—er, lack thereof—if you can get it. Zach Parise, Tyler Myers and Ryan Suter each received $10 million signing bonuses. Parise is a former teammate and linemate of Kovalchuk's—I wonder if he left Kovalchuk a little something, you know, for the effort. Like the way the Dalai Lama left something for Carl in *Caddyshack*.

LET'S PLAY SOME MORE!

GUY CHARRON PLAYED 734 CAREER REGULAR SEASON NHL games without enjoying summer hockey. He holds the record that nobody wants. Jay Bouwmeester played 764 games before seeing playoff action. It looked like his futility streak was going to continue but the Calgary Flames traded him on April Fools' Day in 2013 to the playoff-bound St. Louis Blues. (Wonder if he thought it was a joke at first?) In two playoff series with Bouwmeester, St. Louis has lost them both. So Bouwmeester has never won a playoff series. Participant ribbon material.

THANKS FOR HELPING OUT

WE'VE ALL SEEN GOALS THAT HAVE BEEN UNASSISTED, ONES with one assist, others with two assists. Do I hear three? One time in NHL history a goal was awarded three assists. On February 14, 1931, the Detroit Falcons were playing the Leafs in Toronto. The game ended in a 1–1 tie. The game had been scoreless through two periods until George Hay of the Falcons opened the scoring with an unassisted goal at the 7:50 mark of the third period. A few minutes later Charlie Conacher scored for Toronto. Perhaps referees Odie Cleghorn and Vic Wagner were feeling mighty generous on Valentine's Day, because they gave assists to Busher Jackson, Joe Primeau and King Clancy. It's good to be the King. That makes Clancy the only player in NHL history to be awarded the third assist on an NHL goal. I wonder if Detroit was wondering "our goal was unassisted and they get three?" What's up with that?

BORIS BECKER WOULD BE PROUD

IN THE 2013 NHL SEASON, THE TORONTO MAPLE LEAFS BECAME the first team in league history to have players score who were born in both East Germany and West Germany, respectively. Mikhail Grabovski was born in Potsdam, East Germany (he was raised in Belarus). Korbinian Holzer was born in Munich, West Germany. Holzer scored his first career NHL goal on February 5, 2013. This brings us to a question: who is your favourite hoser? Bob, Doug or Korbinian?

HOME-ICE ADVANTAGE

IF YOU INCLUDE BOTH SUMMIT SERIES AND ALL OF THE CANADA Cups, World Cups and World Junior Championships, Canada has never lost in Toronto or Hamilton. That's a span of 21 games, 20 wins and 1 tie. The tie was against Finland in Toronto in 1991.

LIKE FATHER, LIKE SON

IN MARCH 2012 THE TORONTO MAPLE LEAFS TRADED FOR Carter Ashton, son of former NHLer Brent. Carter wore #37 for the Leafs. The first Leaf to wear #37 was Doug Shedden. Shedden and Brent Ashton were involved in a trade that sent them in opposite directions, with Ashton going to Detroit and taking the #14 that Shedden was wearing. It's an Ashton family tradition to take Shedden's number.

#9 VS #99

GRETZKY VS. HOWE. DID THEY MEET IN THE NHL? IF SO, WHEN, and who did what? They met four times during the 1979–80 season. Here are the details:

NOVEMBER 17—Edmonton 0 at Hartford 4, Howe, one assist
DECEMBER 9—Hartford 0 at Edmonton 3, Gretzky one goal, one assist
JANUARY 2—Hartford 3 at Edmonton 3, Gretzky one assist
FEBRUARY 19—Edmonton 2 at Hartford 6, zero points for both.

In the words of Richard Dawson, "survey says" make that the total, Gretzky one goal, two assists and Howe with one assist. Hartford 2–1–1 in season series.

HE SHOOTS, HE SCORES...

IN THE 2009 PLAYOFFS MARIAN HOSSA SCORED SIX GOALS— two in Game Four against Columbus, two in Game Four against Anaheim and two in Game Four against Chicago. Should have hung a sign on him: BREAK GLASS ONLY IN EVENT OF GAME FOUR.

TRIPLE-GOLD CLUB

THE INTERNATIONAL ICE HOCKEY FEDERATION HAS A...GROUP- ing, I guess would be the best name for it. It includes only players that have won the World Championships, Stanley Cup and Olympics. There are 25 players that have fallen into that category as of the start of the 2014–15 NHL season. I'm not sure if this group gets some kind of commemorative ring or jacket, but they did pose for a picture at the 2010 Olympics. Eight of the players are Canadian: Eric Staal, Scott Niedermayer, Brendan Shanahan, Chris Pronger, Jonathan Toews, Patrice Bergeron, Rob Blake and Joe Sakic. Niedermayer did a couple better than the triple crown. He is the *only* player to win a World Junior Championship (1991), a Memorial Cup (1992), a Stanley Cup (4 times), World Championship (2004), a World Cup (2004) and an Olympic Gold Medal (2002 and 2010). There is one coach in the Triple-Gold Club: Mike Babcock.

HALL OF FAME QUALIFICATIONS

WHAT QUALIFIES A PLAYER TO ENTER THE HOCKEY HALL OF Fame? How about 1,335 points? Out of the 30 players in the history of the NHL that have picked up that many points that are Hall of Fame eligible, only two players are *not* in the Hall of Fame. The players are Mark Recchi (1,533) and Dave Andreychuk (1,338). Logic would dictate that Recchi will get in eventually. Seems like the magic number is 1,335. Players ranked in career points from 31–50, seven of them are not in the Hall of Fame.

WHO'S IN NET? WHERE'S HE FROM?

ON FEBRUARY 18, 2013, DANNY TAYLOR STARTED IN NET FOR the Calgary Flames, making him just the third goalie born in England to start a game in NHL history. Sussex-born Byron Dafoe preceded Taylor, playing over 400 NHL games, lastly in 2004. Chris Worthy, from Bristol, played 26 games in the late 1960s to early '70s.

Bruins in action against the Leafs. These teams only met once in a Stanley Cup Final in 1939. Boston won in five games. PHOTO: COURTESY OF THE BOSTON PUBLIC LIBRARY, LESLIE JONES COLLECTION

SKILLS COMPETITION

NOT QUITE DONE YET. LET'S GO TO A SHOOTOUT. WHO DOESN'T love a shootout? Well I can name a few: Corey Hirsch, the 2006–07 Toronto Maple Leafs and of course Billy Clanton and the McLaury brothers.

Corey Hirsch was the goalie for Canada in the gold medal game in Lillehammer, Norway. Peter Forsberg brought out his bag of tricks for the winning goal, a move that is copied all over the world now. I even did it in air hockey once—I swear to God, as Ovechkin would say.

The Maple Leafs missed the 2007 playoffs thanks to a shootout. And they weren't even involved in it. On the last day of the 2006–07 season the New York Islanders, with Wade Dubielewicz in net, beat New Jersey in a shootout. The Islanders made the playoffs, the Leafs didn't, yadda yadda yadda, which contributed to the Leafs franchise-record seven straight seasons of missing the playoffs

Clanton and the McLaurys were the three killed at the end of the shootout at the O.K. Corral in Tombstone, Arizona. The next shootout in Arizona was on Nov 11, 2005 when the Coyotes lost to the Predators. Three people died at the shootout at the O.K. Coral, there were three Earps also involved. NHL uses three shooters in the shootout. Coincidence?

The longest NHL shootout was one of the first. On November 26, 2005, Rangers and Capitals went through 15 shooters each before Marek Malik scored his epic between the legs goal followed by the hand in the air salute. Still the best shootout goal and reaction of all-time—write that down. That was the only shootout attempt of Malik's career.

In 2014–15 the NHL's leading point scorer, Art Ross winner had the lowest point total since Stan Mikita had 87 points in 67–68. Perhaps the reason for the low point totals in 2014–15, how about 500 fewer power plays than there were in 2013–14. Powers out.

ANOTHER TYPE OF SHOOTOUT

TWO GOALIES IN NHL HISTORY HAVE FACED 73 SHOTS IN A game, while saving 70 of them. The goalies almost shared the same birthday. Roy Worters was born on October 19, 1900 in Toronto, and Ron Tugnutt was born on October 22, 1967 in Toronto. Tugnutt's Nordiques picked up a point as they tied Boston on March 21, 1991. Worter's Pirates lost 3–1 to the Americans on Boxing Day in 1925.

11

ON THIS DATE

LAST CHAPTER. LET'S GO OUT WITH A BANG...YOU KNOW THOSE informative desk calendars—New-Word-a-Day, that sort of thing? Well this follows the same idea but in a convenient one-chapter format! Your daily dose of hockey trivia to get you prepped for the water cooler. Plus, in this chapter I will be observing the leap year, so you get one bonus trivia tidbit.

You learn something new every day.

JANUARY

1 **1973:** Bruins #4 Bobby Orr tied an NHL record by defencemen with six assists in an 8–2 Boston win in Vancouver. Orr tied the record set by Babe Pratt with Toronto in 1944 and tied by Pat Stapleton with Chicago in 1969.

2 **1980:** Gordie Howe became the first player in league history to appear in an NHL game in five different decades, when he played for the Hartford Whalers in Edmonton. The game was a draw, 3–3. No points or penalties for Mr. Hockey.

3   **1991:** Wayne Gretzky became the fourth player in NHL history to score 700 career goals (with his 47th career hat trick) in a 6–3 Kings win on Long Island. Glenn Healy was in net for New York. Gretzky joined Howe, Phil Esposito and Marcel Dionne. Mike Gartner, Brett Hull and Jaromir Jagr would later join the 700 Club.

4   **1944:** Montreal and Toronto set an NHL record for fastest six goals by two teams (3:15). Canadiens scored four of the six and won 6–3 at the Forum.

5   **1910:** The Montreal Canadiens of the NHA played their first game in team history. It took place before 5,000 fans at the Jubilee Rink. Fans got their money's worth on opening night as Montreal won 7–6 in overtime against Cobalt.

6   **1993:** Wayne Gretzky played in his first game of the 1992–93 season, and the 1,000th of his NHL career. He picked up two assists as his L.A. Kings lost at home to Tampa Bay 6–3.

7   **1997:** The Philadelphia Flyers ran their undefeated streak to 17 games (14–0–3) with a win at home against Boston. Eric Lindros had at least a point in each of the 17 games (13 goals, 16 assists total). The streak ended two days later at home against Tampa Bay.

8   **1990:** Mario Lemieux extended his point-scoring streak to 31 games with his 24th career hat trick (4 goals) as his Penguins won 7–5 at Madison Square Garden. Lemieux played in 59 games that season; he had points in 54 games.

The Canadiens and the Maple Leafs have not met in the playoffs since 1979. PHOTO: LIBRARY AND ARCHIVES CANADA/CREDIT: FRANK PRAZAK/ WEEKEND MAGAZINE FONDS/EOO2505692

9   **1981:** As a member of the New York Rangers, Phil Esposito played in his final NHL game, a 3–3 tie against the Sabres in the Big Apple. Esposito retired as the second-highest scorer in NHL history (behind only Gordie Howe). Esposito assisted on a goal by Dean Talafous that opened the scoring.

10   **1989:** Wayne Gretzky became the NHL's all-time leading scorer in combined regular season and playoff points, with a total of 2,011, passing Gordie Howe. It came in a 5–4 overtime win against Gretzky's old team, Edmonton. Gretzky had four assists in the game.

11   **1976:** The Philadelphia Flyers beat the touring Soviet Army Team 4–1 at the Spectrum in Philadelphia. It was the Soviet Army's first loss on the tour. It was the infamous "they're going home" game.

12   **1918:** The Montreal Canadiens' Joe Malone scored five times to become the first 20-goal scorer in NHL history as the Canadiens won 9–4 over Ottawa. Newsy Lalonde scored twice in the game, to give him 15 goals on the season.

13   **1982:** Edmonton's rookie goalie Grant Fuhr extended his unbeaten streak to 23 straight games (15–0–8) when the Oilers tied the Capitals 6–6 in Washington. Edmonton had a 4–1 lead in the game. Dennis Maruk tied the game with 10 seconds remaining in the third period.

14   **1922:** Montreal defenceman Sprague Cleghorn and his brother Odie each scored four goals as they led the Canadiens to a 10–6 win over the Hamilton Tigers in Montreal. It gave both players seven goals on the season.

15   **1841:** Lord Frederick Stanley, for whom the Stanley Cup is named, was born in England. He was Canada's Governor General from 1888 to 1893.

16   **1905:** "One-Eyed" Frank McGee scored a Stanley Cup record 14 goals in the Ottawa Silver Seven's 23–2 win over the Dawson City Nuggets, who had travelled more than 6,000 kilometres by dogsled, boat and train.

17   **1962:** Chicago Black Hawks goaltender Glenn Hall played in his 500th consecutive game (including the playoffs). Chicago beat the Rangers 3–1, and Hall made 24 saves.

18   **1958:** New Brunswick native Willie O'Ree played in Montreal and became the first black player to appear in an NHL game. He went pointless as the Bruins beat the Canadiens 3–0. Harry Lumley with the shutout.

19   **1996:** NHL Board of Governors approved the sale of the Winnipeg Jets, officially clearing the way for the team to move to Phoenix, Arizona in time for the 1996–97 season. Approval came during the NHL All-Star break.

20   **1982:** Toronto traded Darryl Sittler to the Philadelphia Flyers in exchange for Rich Costello, a second-round draft pick in 1982 (Peter Ihnacak) and future considerations (Ken Strong). (Probably should have put Costello and Strong in the "Who Are These Guys?" chapter.)

21   **1887:** Georges Vezina was born in Chicoutimi, Quebec. Vezina played in the NHL 1917–18 through 1925–26 with the Montreal Canadiens.

22   **1987:** A snowstorm in New Jersey delayed the start of the Devils and Flames game for two hours. There were just 334 fans were on hand to see the Devils beat the Flames 7–5. The game ended just before midnight.

23 **1993:** Mike Gartner became the first player in NHL history to score 30 goals in 14 consecutive seasons. He scored the Rangers eighth goal in an 8–3 win over the Kings in L.A. on Robb Stauber.

24 **1971:** Boston's Bobby Orr extended his consecutive-game point-scoring streak to 18 (nine goals, 26 assists), with a goal and two assists in the Bruins' 4–2 win over Montreal in Boston. Orr scored his 20th goal of the season in the game.

25 **1986:** Edmonton's Paul Coffey set an NHL record for de-fencemen with a point in his 28th straight game, when the Oilers won 5–2 over the visiting L.A. Kings. The assist came on a second-period goal by Mark Napier.

26 **1961:** Wayne Douglas Gretzky was born in Brantford, Ontario. That night, Gordie Howe scored his 467th career NHL goal on Glenn Hall, as Detroit and Chicago tied 2–2. Quite the head start Mr. Hockey had on The Great One.

27 **1984:** Wayne Gretzky extended his NHL-record consecu-tive-point streak to 51 games in a 3–3 Oilers tie with New Jersey. He scored in the first period on Ron Low. The streak began on opening night October 5, 1983. In total, Gretzky scored 61 goals and 92 assists in the 51 games.

28 **1960:** Montreal's Jean Beliveau recorded his 500th career NHL point (a goal) in his 424th career game. Beliveau had one goal and one assist in the Canadiens 4–2 win in Detroit. Sawchuk was in net for the Red Wings.

29 **1977:** The Blizzard of 1977 left many Buffalo Sabres trapped in Buffalo including Lee Fogolin, Jim Lorentz, Brian Spencer and Richard Martin. Only 14 players made it to Montreal, but they managed to tie the Canadiens, 3–3. Ted Darling, the Sabres play-by-play man for radio and TV, called the game on the telephone from his home in Lockport, New York. Sabres trailed the game 2–0 in the second period.

30 **2004:** Chicago Blackhawks ended their team-record road losing streak of 19 straight games, when two goals from rookie Tuomo Ruutu gave them a 5–3 win over the Flames in Calgary. Flames led 3–2 at the end of two periods. One of the 19 losses was in overtime. Chicago had an overall winless streak of 14 games that season.

31 **1976:** The L.A. Kings ended Montreal's 43-game West Coast unbeaten streak (against Kings, Seals and Canucks), with a 7–3 win in L.A. The Kings scored three goals in 57 seconds in the second period to break a 3–3 tie to take a 6–3 lead. They added another goal in the third period.

FEBRUARY

1 **1993:** New NHL Commissioner Gary Bettman officially took office. First order of business: water the plants. Bettman would see more work stoppages as Commissioner than any other leader in pro sports.

2 **1994:** Scotty Bowman picked up his 1,000th coaching victory (regular season and playoff) as the Red Wings won 3–1 over the Lightning in Tampa Bay. Bowman would end up with over 1,400 career wins (regular and post-season). No other coach has over 1,000.

Darryl Sittler holds the NHL record for most points in a game: ten. He had six goals and four assists against the Bruins on February 7, 1976. PHOTO: CITY OF TORONTO ARCHIVES, FONDS 1257, SERIES 1057, ITEM 4253

3 **1973:** Montreal's rookie defenceman Larry Robinson scored his first NHL goal in a 7–1 Canadiens win over the Kings, at Los Angeles. Robinson scored the opening goal of the game on Rogie Vachon. Guy Lapointe and Frank Mahovlich assisted on the goal. Robinson finished his career with the Kings and scored in his final game.

4 **1943:** Frank Calder, president of the NHL since its inception in 1917, died of a heart attack at the age of 65 in Montreal. He's buried in Mount Royal Cemetery in Montreal.

5 **1950:** Montreal's Dick Irvin became the first coach in NHL history to win 500 games when the Canadiens beat the Bruins 5–3 at the Forum in Montreal. George Boucher was the head coach of Boston that night in the only season he ever coached in the NHL.

6 **1890:** Hall of Famer Harry Cameron born in Pembroke, Ontario. Cameron played in the NHL 1917–18 through 1922–23. He was the first player with a goal, an assist and a fight in one NHL game.

7 **1976:** Darryl Sittler set an NHL record for points in a game with 10. He had six goals and four assists at home against Boston. He had a hat trick in each of the second and third periods.

8 **1942:** Chicago rookie Bill Mosienko scored two goals in 21 seconds in his first game. Ten years later, Mosienko had three goals in 21 seconds. Better with age.

9 **1966:** Expansion era began as the NHL announced that six conditional franchises had been granted to Los Angeles, San Francisco, St. Louis, Philadelphia, Pittsburgh and Minneapolis for the 1967–68 season. The teams would all form one conference/division. Meaning one of them would make the Stanley Cup Final.

The "Kraut Line"—#17 Bobby Bauer, #15 Milt Schmidt and #14 Woody Dumart. PHOTO: COURTESY OF THE BOSTON PUBLIC LIBRARY, LESLIE JONES COLLECTION

10 **1942:** In their final game before joining the Royal Canadian Air Force, the "Kraut Line" of Schmidt, Bauer and Dumart had 11 points and led Boston to an 8–1 win over Montreal. Afterwards, they were carried off the ice by players from both teams.

11 **1922:** After 20 minutes of overtime, the Toronto St. Pats and Ottawa Senators settled for a 4–4 tie at Ottawa. It was the first game in NHL history that ended in a tie. Toronto scored twice in the third period to tie the game. John Ross Roach, the St. Pats goalie, faced 82 shots in the 80-minute game.

12 **1949:** Canada beat Denmark 47–0 at the World Championships in Stockholm, Sweden in the most lopsided international hockey game in history.

13 **1993:** Doug Gilmour had six assists to lead the Maple Leafs to a 6–1 win against the Minnesota North Stars in Toronto. Gilmour's six assists tied a Maple Leafs record set by Babe Pratt. The assists came in the fourth game of a nine-game assist streak for Gilmour, he had 24 assists in that span.

14 **1927:** The Toronto Maple Leafs were born when Conn Smythe purchased the Toronto St. Pats franchise and renamed the team and changed the colours. The Maple Leafs played their first game three days later.

15 **1946:** The NHL reinstated Babe Pratt of the Toronto Maple Leafs, who had been expelled from the league because of gambling. Pratt ended up missing five games.

16 **1923:** Broadcasting legend Foster Hewitt called his first hockey game. Hewitt used a telephone to broadcast the Ontario Hockey Association game in Toronto on CFCA radio.

17 **1982:** Gilbert Perreault became Buffalo's all-time leading goal scorer when the Sabres won 3–2 at Chicago. His 383rd career goal as a Sabre put him one ahead of Rick Martin. It was the game-winning goal, scored in the third period on Tony Esposito.

18 **1930:** Boston set a new NHL record for most wins in a season with their 31st of the year (and their 16th straight at home) in a 3–2 victory over the Montreal Maroons. The Bruins broke the old record of 30 wins, set by Ottawa in 1926–27. Bruins would win seven of their final eight games after that. Their lone loss came in OT.

19 **1980:** Edmonton rookie Wayne Gretzky played against Hartford's Gordie Howe for the fourth (and final) time in their NHL careers, when the Whalers beat the Oilers 6–2 at Hartford. Both players went scoreless in the game.

20 **2013:** Buffalo Sabres fired head coach Lindy Ruff. Ruff had been coach since July 21, 1997, coaching a total of 1,165 games. Ruff's 571 wins were second to Al Arbour (740) for most with one team. At the time Gregg Popovich, coach of the NBA's San Antonio Spurs, was the only head coach in the four major pro sports in North America with longer active tenure.

21 **1974:** Defenceman Tim Horton of the Sabres died in an automobile accident driving back to Buffalo after a game in Toronto. Horton's Ford Pantera flipped over on the highway in St. Catharine's, Ontario in the early hours of the morning.

22 **1956:** In his first full season in the NHL the New York Rangers' Lou Fontinato set a new NHL single-season penalty-minute record. His 169 penalty minutes broke the old record of 167 set by Red Horner in 1935–36. Fontinato tied the record with a first-period fight and then broke the record in the second period with a roughing minor.

23 **1952:** Montreal's Elmer Lach became the NHL's all-time scoring leader when he had a goal and three assists in a 7–0 win over Chicago. The four points gave Lach 550 career NHL points, two more than Bill Cowley, who had held the record since 1946.

24 **1980:** United States Olympic hockey team defeated Finland, 4–2 to win the 1980 Gold Medal at the Lake Placid Winter Olympics.

25 **1971:** Boston set an NHL record for the fastest three goals by a team. En route to an 8–3 win over the Canucks, John Bucyk, Ed Westfall and Ted Green scored goals in 20 seconds in the third period. Bruins scored a total of six goals in the third period, including a hat trick by Bucyk.

Lou Fontinato had a legendary fight with Gordie Howe—legendary because Howe beat him up badly. PHOTO: LIBRARY AND ARCHIVES CANADA/ CREDIT: LOUIS JAQUES/WEEKEND MAGAZINE FONDS/E002505664

26 **1955:** Doug Harvey picked up his 41st assist of the season to set a new NHL record for assists by a defenceman, as the Canadiens won 4–1 over the Bruins, at the Forum. Harvey surpassed the old mark of 40 set by Toronto's Babe Pratt in 1943–44. The assist came on a first period power-play goal by Maurice Richard.

27 **1877:** The *Montreal Gazette* published the first formal rules of hockey in an article entitled "Hockey on Ice." Most of the rules have changed in 100+ years, but scoring goals remains the same.

28 **2010:** Sidney Crosby scores the "Golden Goal" at the Olympics in Vancouver. Canada defeated the U.S. 3–2 in OT after Zach Parise had tied the game with 25 seconds remaining in third period.

The Golden Goal. Sidney Crosby scores Olympic gold-medal-winning OT goal on Ryan Miller. PHOTO: AP-CHRIS O'MEARA/THE CANADIAN PRESS

Canada celebrates Crosby's OT winning shot in the gold medal game against the United States. PHOTO: S.YUME/FLICKR

29 **1936:** Hall of Famer Henri Richard was born in Montreal. The Pocket Rocket, younger brother of Maurice, Henri Richard would win 11 Stanley Cups as a player, more than anyone else in NHL history.

MARCH

1 **1988:** Wayne Gretzky of the Oilers picked up his 1,050th assist in the first period of a game against the Kings, moving ahead of Gordie Howe as the NHL's all-time leader in career assists.

2 **1918:** Toronto beat Montreal 5–3, as the Canadiens' Joe Malone finished the first NHL season with 44 goals in 22 games, a league record which stood until 1944–45 when Maurice Richard scored 50. Malone did not score in the game.

3 **1875:** The earliest recorded ice hockey game was played. It featured McGill University against the Victoria Skating Club at the Victoria Rink in Montreal. The two teams played with nine men on a side and used a flat, thin disk as a puck. Some reports indicated a cow's kneecap was used. I didn't know cows had kneecaps.

4 **1941:** Boston set an NHL record with 83 shots on goal against Chicago goalie Sam LoPresti in a 3–2 win over the visiting Black Hawks. The Bruins also set a record with 37 shots in the first period. Bill Cowley of Boston had two assists in the game to set a single season assist record of 38, one more than Joe Primeau of the Leafs who accomplished that in 1931–32.

The Bruins won their first Stanley Cup in their fifth NHL season in 1928-29.
PHOTO: COURTESY OF THE BOSTON PUBLIC LIBRARY, LESLIE JONES COLLECTION

5 **1963:** Detroit's Gordie Howe scored a goal to become the first player in NHL history to score 1,200 career points. The milestone came in his 1,112th regular season game, a 4–3 loss to the Canadiens in Detroit. Howe opened the scoring midway through the first period.

6 **2004:** Mike Sillinger became just the third player in NHL history to play for 10 different teams during his career, when he appeared in his first game with the St. Louis Blues. He picked up two assists in the game.

7 **1998:** The Rangers' Wayne Gretzky scored his 1,000th career NHL goal (878 regular season and 122 more in the playoffs) as New York lost 6–3 at New Jersey. The goal was scored on Martin Brodeur in the second period and tied the game 3–3.

8 **1937:** Montreal's Howie Morenz died just six weeks after suffering a broken leg during a game against Chicago. Morenz died in a Montreal hospital.

9 **1948:** NHL President Clarence Campbell expelled New York's Billy Taylor and suspended Boston's Don Gallinger for gambling associations. They were alleged to have bet on hockey games, though none were "fixed." Taylor was reinstated in 1970.

10 **2004:** The Edmonton Oilers set an NHL record by playing in their sixth consecutive overtime game, a 3–2 loss to the visiting Colorado Avalanche. Edmonton was 2–2–2 in that stretch and would lose in overtime in their next game to Vancouver.

11 **1918:** The first all-NHL Stanley Cup playoff game took place as the Toronto Blueshirts hosted the Montreal Canadiens in the first of their two-game, total-goal series. Toronto beat the Canadiens 7–3. Harry Meeking had a hat trick for Toronto. Montreal won the next game 4–3 at home. Toronto advanced to the final against Vancouver.

12 **1972:** Goaltender Gerry Cheevers extended his NHL-record unbeaten streak to 28 straight games (21–0–7), in the Bruins 4–4 tie against Pittsburgh. Penguins scored two goals in a nine-second span in the third period to tie the game.

13 **1955:** Montreal's Maurice "Rocket" Richard was ejected during a 4–2 Canadiens loss to Boston. Richard had a fight late in the third period against Hal Laycoe. Richard hit Laycoe over the head with his stick and was ejected for attempt to injure. Richard also punched a linesman.

14 **1962:** Detroit's Gordie Howe became the second player in NHL history to get 500 career goals. #500 came in Howe's 1,045th career game.

15 **1970:** Boston's Bobby Orr scored two goals and added two assists to become the first defenceman (and fourth player) in NHL history to get 100 points in a season.

16 **1955:** Montreal's Maurice Richard was suspended by President Clarence Campbell for the remainder of the NHL season and the playoffs after striking a linesman in a game at Boston. (*See* March 13, above.)

17 **1955:** A riot erupted in Montreal, as fans protested NHL President Clarence Campell's suspension of Maurice Richard. The Canadiens forfeited the game to the Red Wings after a smoke bomb went off in the Forum.

18 **1945:** In the final game of the 1944–45 season at Boston, Maurice Richard became the first player in NHL history to score 50 goals in one season. Richard scored his 50 goals in just 50 games.

19 **1933:** The first day game in NHL history was played between the Red Wings and Black Hawks at Chicago. The starting time was 3:30 p.m. The Red Wings won 4–2. Even worse news for Chicago: Billy Burch broke his leg crashing into boards, ending his career.

20 **1971:** NHL history was made as two brothers faced each other in goal for the first time ever. Ken Dryden's Canadiens beat Dave Dryden's Sabres 5–2 at the Montreal Forum. Ken came in to replace an injured Rogie Vachon. Dave didn't last too much longer after that as he was pulled after allowing three goals.

21 **1970:** Minnesota's Charlie Burns became the final player-coach to score a goal in a regular season NHL game when he tallied once in a 5–4 North Stars win against Eddie Johnston of the visiting Boston Bruins.

22 **1934:** Herbie Lewis scored the first power-play OT goal in NHL history, 1:33 into the extra frame, to give the Red Wings a 2–1 win in Toronto for Game One of the Stanley Cup Semifinals. It was the first OT goal in the Red Wings playoff history. Hap Day was in the penalty box for Toronto. He received a tripping penalty with 20 seconds left in regulation.

23 **1918:** Alf Skinner of Toronto scored the first hat trick by an NHL player in the Stanley Cup Final. It didn't help, as his Arenas lost to Vancouver 6–4.

24 **1982:** Rick Vaive became the first 50-goal scorer in Toronto Maple Leafs history when he scored in a 4–3 win against the visiting St. Louis Blues. The goal came on the power play in the first period on Mike Liut.

25 **1997:** Hartford Whalers announced that they would move from Connecticut to North Carolina following the 1996–97 season. Whalers lost 4–0 that night; it was their sixth straight loss.

26 **1997:** The NHL announced that the Anaheim Mighty Ducks and Vancouver Canucks would open the 1997–98 season with two games in Japan, the first regular-season games in league history played outside North America.

27 **1993:** Sherry Ross of WABC radio in New York became the first woman in NHL history to do play-by-play of a game when she handled the first period of the 5–2 New Jersey Devils win over the Washington Capitals.

28 **1999:** Colorado's Patrick Roy became the NHL's all-time winningest goaltender (regular season plus playoffs) with his 7–2 win over the visiting L.A. Kings. The victory gave him 506 career wins. Theo Fleury had the game-winning goal for the Avalanche.

29 **1973:** The Flyers' Bobby Clarke became the first player from a post-1967 expansion team (and the ninth player in NHL history) to score 100 points in a season. His 100th point was a goal against Phil Myre of the Atlanta Flames. Clarke scored twice in the game. The Flyers won 4–2 at the Spectrum in Philadelphia.

30 **1916:** Montreal Canadiens won their first Stanley Cup, defeating the Portland Rosebuds of the Pacific Coast Hockey Association 2–1 in the fifth and deciding game.

31 **1928:** Gordie Howe was born in Floral, Saskatchewan. Mr. Hockey spent most of his NHL career with the Red Wings. Howe would hold many NHL records before Wayne Gretzky came along.

APRIL

1 **1919:** The final game for the 1919 Stanley Cup was cancelled because of an influenza epidemic sweeping North America. The Canadiens' Joe Hall died.

2 **1989:** Calgary's Joey Mullen set a new NHL record for most points in a season by a U.S.-born player, when his goal and two assists in a 4–2 win over the Oilers gave him 110 points on the final day of the regular season.

3 **1997:** Wayne Gretzky notched his 2,700th career NHL point with a goal on Jim Carey in a 5–4 Rangers win over Boston. The point gave Gretzky a lead of 850 points over Gordie Howe in career NHL scoring. Messier, who also scored in the game, would end up second behind Gretzky.

4 **1971:** Gordie Howe appeared in his 1,687th (and final) regular season game with the Detroit Red Wings, as the Rangers beat Detroit 6–0 at New York. Ed Giacomin had the shutout for New York.

5 **1991:** Jaromir Jagr scores his first career playoff goal. A big one it was: overtime winner for the Penguins against New Jersey.

6 **1980:** Hartford's 52-year-old Gordie Howe scored his 801st (and final) NHL goal. It came in the second period against Detroit goaltender Rogie Vachon. It came on the final day of the season.

7 **2002:** Jarome Iginla scored twice to become the first (and only) 50-goal scorer of the 2001–02 season, in the Flames 3–2 loss to the Blackhawks in Chicago.

8 **1978:** Guy Lafleur scored his 59th and 60th goals of the year on Ron Low to lead Montreal to a 5–1 win over the visiting Red Wings. Lafleur became the second Canadiens player to score 60 goals in a season. The goals came in the second to last game of the season.

9 **1997:** Brett Hull scored his 500th goal as a member of the Blues, while goaltender Grant Fuhr made 23 saves for his 20th career shutout in the Blues 1–0 win, at Chicago. Hull scored on Jeff Hackett.

10 **1993:** The Ottawa Senators ended their NHL-record 38-game road losing streak with a 5–3 win over the Islanders at New York. It was their only road win of the season. Ottawa scored three goals in the third period, including the winner by Laurie Boschman with 56 seconds remaining.

11 **1981:** Edmonton's Wayne Gretzky scored the first hat trick in Oilers playoff history against Richard Sevigny, and added an assist as the Oilers won 6–2 over the visiting Montreal Canadiens, in Game Three of the preliminary round.

12 **1945:** Toronto Maple Leafs rookie goalie Frank McCool set a new Stanley Cup record with his third consecutive playoff shutout, in a 1–0 win over Detroit in the final. The win gave Toronto a 3–0 series lead. Detroit would win the next three games to tie the series. Toronto won game seven.

13 **1985:** Tim Kerr scored four goals in 8 minutes and 16 seconds in the second period to set an NHL playoff record for most goals in one period as the Flyers beat the Rangers, 6–5 in Game Three of the Patrick Division Semifinals. Kerr also tied an NHL record with three power-play goals. The consecutive goals were on Glenn Hanlon.

14 **2003:** Patrick Roy picked up his 150th career playoff victory, and his 23rd playoff shutout, as the Avalanche won 3–0 against the Wild at Minnesota in Game Three of the Western Conference Quarterfinals. Roy became the first goalie to get 150 playoff wins.

15 **1998:** Tie Domi set a Toronto Maple Leafs record for most penalty minutes in a season, when his 17 penalty minutes (in a 3–2 win over the visiting Chicago Blackhawks) broke the season record of 351 set by Dave "Tiger" Williams in 1977–78.

16 **1992:** Mike Gartner picked up his 500th career NHL assist in a 7–1 Rangers win over Pittsburgh to become the first player in NHL history to get his 500th goal, 500th assist, 1,000th point and 1,000th NHL game all in the same season.

17 **1995:** The L.A. Kings' Wayne Gretzky picked up an assist to become the first 2,500-career-point scorer in NHL history as L.A. lost 5–2 at Calgary.

18 **1942:** Toronto completed the greatest comeback in playoff history with their fourth straight win, a 3–1 victory over Detroit, in Game Seven of the Stanley Cup Final. Leafs goalie Turk Broda allowed the Red Wings just seven goals in the final four games.

Walter "Turk" Broda was inducted into the Hockey Hall of Fame in 1967. He played his entire 629-game NHL career with Toronto. PHOTO: COURTESY OF THE BOSTON PUBLIC LIBRARY, LESLIE JONES COLLECTION

19 **1970:** Phil Esposito scored a hat trick as the Bruins won 6–3 at Chicago, in Game One of the Stanley Cup Semifinals. Brother Tony Esposito was in goal for the Blackhawks.

20 **1969:** Bobby Orr scored his first Stanley Cup–playoff goal, the game winner, as the Bruins won 3–2 over the Montreal Canadiens, in Game Four of their Stanley Cup Semifinal series, in Boston.

21 **1978:** In a World Hockey Association game at Edmonton, Hartford's Gordie Howe scored on the first shift, just minutes after finding out that he had become a grandfather. Mark and Ginger Howe's first son Travis made Gordie the first active grandpa in pro-hockey history.

22 **1990:** The L.A. Kings set a team playoff record for fastest two goals, when Larry Robinson and Todd Elik scored just 11 seconds apart in the first period in Game Three of the Smythe Division Final against Edmonton in L.A. Kings lost 5–4 to the Oilers.

23 **1964:** Toronto Maple Leafs Bobby Baun scored the overtime winning goal at 1:43 while playing on a broken leg to defeat the Red Wings 4–3 in Game Six of the Final. Leafs won again two nights later to win the Stanley Cup.

24 **1979:** The Rangers and Flyers set an NHL playoff record for most goals in one period with nine in the third period. There were nine different goal scorers as well. New York won the period 6–3 and the game 8–3, in Game Five of the quarterfinals. The Rangers eventually won the series in five games.

25 **1998:** Jaromir Jagr picked up an assist to give him 100 career points in 100 NHL playoff games. The milestone came in the Penguins 4–1 win over Montreal in Game Two of the Eastern Conference Quarterfinals.

26 **1977:** Montreal played their 38th straight home game without a loss (including four playoff wins)—an NHL record. Ken Dryden's sixth career playoff shutout gave the Canadiens a 3–0 win over the visiting Islanders in Game Two of the semifinal round. Including playoffs, Montreal lost twice at home that season.

27 **1998:** St. Louis blueliner Chris Pronger had three assists in a span of two minutes when the Blues scored four power-play goals in three minutes and seven seconds in the third period (fastest four power-play goals in NHL history) to come from a 3–0 deficit for a 4–3 win at L.A., in Game Three of the Western Conference Quarterfinals. At 8:34 of the third period L.A. defencemen Sean O'Donnell received five minutes for fighting; no one on St. Louis received a penalty.

28 **2001:** Patrick Roy became the NHL's all-time leader with 16 career playoff shutouts (breaking the mark of 15 set by Clint Benedict) as the Avalanche won 2–0 against the visiting Kings in Game Two of the Western Conference Semifinals.

29 **1993:** Dino Ciccarelli of Detroit became the first player in history to score a playoff hat trick with three different teams, when he scored 3 times, all on the power play, in a 7–3 win at Toronto. Ciccarelli had earlier playoff hat tricks with the Minnesota North Stars and Washington.

30 **1972:** Ken Hodge scored his only playoff hat trick and Garnet "Ace" Bailey scored the winner to lead the Bruins to a 6–5 win over the Rangers in Game One of the Stanley Cup Final. It was the first time in 43 years that Boston met New York in the Final. Boston beat the Rangers in 1929 in just a two-game final.

MAY

1 **1992:** Buffalo's Pat LaFontaine became the first player in NHL history to score a goal in each of his team's first seven playoff games in one year. The milestone came in a 3–2 Sabres loss at Boston, in Game Seven of the Adams Division Semifinals. LaFontaine had eight goals in the seven games.

2 **1967:** Toronto beat Montreal 3–1 in Game Six of the Final to become the 1967 Stanley Cup Champions. It was the last Stanley Cup Final series between the so-called Original Six teams.

3 **1995:** Jaromir Jagr became the first European player to lead the NHL in scoring as the Penguins lost 4–3 to the visiting Panthers. Jagr and Philadelphia's Eric Lindros ended up tied with 70 points apiece in the shortened 48-game season but Jagr led in goals, 32–29. Ten of the next 16 NHL scoring champions were European, including Jagr four times.

4 **1972:** Bobby Orr scored a goal to break the career record for playoff goals by a defencemen. His 17th came in only his 47th playoff game. He broke the mark set by Detroit's Red Kelly (16) in 94 playoff games. Boston lost to the Rangers, 5–2 at New York. Orr's goal came in the second period on Ed Giacomin.

5 **1966:** Henri Richard scored the game winner at 2:20 of OT (the only OT goal of his playoff career) on Roger Crozier, 2:20 into the extra period as Montreal beat Detroit 3–2 in Game Six to win the 1966 Stanley Cup.

6 **1976:** Reggie Leach scored five times (to tie a record set by Maurice Richard), and extended his goal-scoring streak to nine games (breaking Maurice Richard's record) as the Flyers beat the Bruins 6–3 at the Spectrum, to win their semifinal series in five games.

7 **1993:** Wayne Gretzky set a record with his 19th career playoff game-winning goal in the Kings' 7–4 win over the Canucks, in Game Three of the Smythe Division Final in L.A. Gretzky broke Maurice Richard's record of 18 career playoff game-winning goals. Gretzky would add two more game-winning goals in the '93 playoffs, both against Toronto.

8 **1973:** Chicago and Montreal combined to set an NHL record with 15 goals in one Stanley Cup Final game, including eight in the second period. Black Hawks won 8–7 in Game Five, at Montreal. Stan Mikita scored two goals and added two assists for the Black Hawks.

9 **1978:** Ken Dryden recorded his 10th (and final) career playoff shutout as the Canadiens won 2–0 at Toronto in Game Four of the Stanley Cup Semifinals. It gave the Habs a sweep over the Leafs and their eighth consecutive road victory (over two seasons). They would lose their next two road playoff games, both in Boston.

10 **1970:** Bobby Orr's overtime goal at 0:40 gave Boston a 4–3 win over St. Louis, and gave the Bruins the 1970 Stanley Cup in four straight games over the Blues. Orr won the Conn Smythe Trophy as playoff MVP. That was the third straight Stanley Cup Final the Blues were swept in.

11 **1972:** Boston beat the New York Rangers 3–0 in Game Six of the Final to win the 1972 Stanley Cup. Gerry Cheevers notched the shutout. Bobby Orr became the fourth player to score two Cup-winning goals in his career and the first to win the Conn Smythe Trophy twice.

12 **2001:** Joe Sakic scored twice, including the winning goal on a penalty shot in the second period and added two assists as the Avalanche won 4–1 against the visiting St. Louis Blues in Game One of the Western Conference Finals. The goals came on Roman Turek.

13 **1980:** Denis Potvin scored (with one second remaining in a power play) at 4:07 of OT to give the Islanders a 4–3 win over the Flyers in Game One of the 1980 Stanley Cup Final. It was the first OT power-play goal in Stanley Cup Final history. Jimmy Watson was in the penalty box for the Flyers.

14 **1977:** Jacques Lemaire scored twice, including the winner at 4:32 of OT to lead the Canadiens to a 2–1 win at Boston in Game Four of the Final. Montreal swept the 1977 Stanley Cup in four games, their 20th Stanley Cup title.

15 **1995:** Vancouver set an NHL playoff record for fastest two shorthanded goals by one team, when Christian Ruuttu and Geoff Courtnall scored within a 17-second span during a 6–5 win over the Blues in Game Five of the Western Conference Quarterfinals. Tim Hunter was in the penalty box for Vancouver.

16 **1982:** The New York Islanders became the first U.S.-based team to win three straight Stanley Cups when Mike Bossy scored twice, both in the second period, in a 3–1 Game Four victory in Vancouver. Bossy scored 17 goals in the playoffs that year.

17 **1979:** Ken Dryden became the first goalie in NHL history to pick up a point in the Stanley Cup Final. He drew an assist on Jacques Lemaire's goal at 17:10 of the third period to give the Canadiens a 4–1 win over the Rangers in Game Three.

18 **1971:** Jean Beliveau played his final game in the NHL as Montreal beat Chicago 3–2 in Game Seven of the Stanley Cup Final. The win gave Montreal their 17th Stanley Cup title. Beliveau had no points in the game.

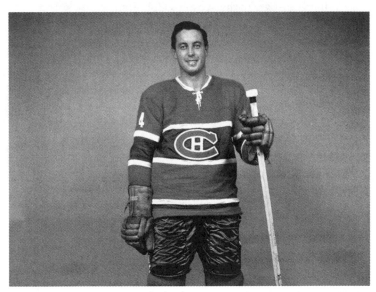

Mr. Beliveau was inducted into the Hockey Hall of Fame in 1972. He died in December 2014. PHOTO: LIBRARY AND ARCHIVES CANADA/CREDIT: LOUIS JAQUES/WEEKEND MAGAZINE FONDS/E002505663

19 **1974:** Philadelphia became the first modern expansion team to win the Stanley Cup, beating Boston 1–0 in Game Six. Rick MacLeish scored the game's only goal, while goalie Bernie Parent won the Conn Smythe Trophy with his second career playoff shutout.

20 **1975:** Fog rolled in at the Aud in Buffalo, delaying Game Three of the Stanley Cup Final between the Sabres and Flyers. At one point Jim Lorentz killed a bat with his stick, before Rene Roberts' OT goal at 18:29 won it for the Sabres 5–4. Sabres replaced goalie Gerry Desjardins after he allowed three goals on six shots in the first period.

21 **1981:** Butch Goring scored twice as the New York Islanders beat the Minnesota North Stars 5–1 in Game Five of the Final to win the 1981 Stanley Cup, their second straight championship. Goring won the Conn Smythe Trophy as playoff MVP.

22 **1978:** Bobby Hull scored the winning goal as the Winnipeg Jets beat the New England Whalers 5–3 in Game Four of the final to win the 1978 Avco Cup as World Hockey Association Champions. Robert Guindon was named Finals MVP.

23 **1992:** Mario Lemieux scored twice to lead the Penguins to a 5–1 win at Boston, and a four-game sweep of the Bruins in the Wales Conference Finals. Lemieux had four goals and four assists while playing in three games in the series.

24 **1988:** The lights went out in Boston at 16:37 of the second period (due to a power outage) with the game tied 3–3 between the Bruins and the Oilers in Game Four of the Stanley Cup Final. The scoring totals counted, but the game was not. Edmonton won the following game at home, for a four-game sweep in the series.

25 **1989:** Calgary Flames beat the Canadiens 4–2 to win the 1989 Stanley Cup. It was the first time since 1928 that the Canadiens lost the last game of the Final on home ice (Rangers won at the Forum against the Maroons in 1928).

26 **1977:** Quebec Nordiques defeated the Winnipeg Jets 8–2 to win the 1977 Avco Cup. Serge Bernier was named playoff MVP. The Jets won three titles in a four year span.

27 **1975:** Bernie Parent shutout Buffalo 2–0 (his sixth and final career playoff shutout) in Game Six of the Final, as the Flyers won their second straight Stanley Cup. Parent became the first back-to-back winner of the Conn Smythe Trophy.

28 **2003:** Patrick Roy announced his retirement after 18 NHL seasons with Montreal and Colorado. Roy retired as the NHL's all-time leader with 1,029 regular season games, 551 wins, 247 Stanley Cup playoff games, 151 playoff victories and 20 playoff shutouts.

29 **1993:** Wayne Gretzky set a Stanley Cup record, with his eighth career playoff hat trick, and added an assist to lead the Kings to a 5–4 win at Toronto in Game Seven of the Campbell Conference Finals. The win advanced the Kings to the Stanley Cup Final.

30 **1999:** Chris Drury scored two goals, including his fourth game winner of the playoffs (to tie an NHL rookie record held by Claude Lemieux), as Colorado won 7–5 at Dallas, in Game Five of the Western Conference Finals. Drury had 47 career playoff goals, 17 were game winners.

31 **2001:** 40-year-old Ray Bourque became the oldest player to score a goal in the Stanley Cup Final as the Avalanche won 3–1 against the Devils in Game Three of the Stanley Cup Final in New Jersey. Bourque's goal was a power-play game winner in the third. It was the fourth and final game-winning goal in his playoff career.

JUNE

1 **1992:** Pittsburgh Penguins beat Chicago 6–5 in Game Four of the Final to become the 1992 Stanley Cup Champions. The win gave the Penguins 11 straight playoff victories and two consecutive Stanley Cups. Dirk Graham had a hat trick for Chicago in the loss.

2 **2001:** Patrik Elias scored a goal and an assist as the Devils scored twice in the final 12 minutes of the third period for a 3–2 victory against the visiting Colorado Avalanche in Game Four of the Stanley Cup Final to tie the series 2–2. New Jersey outshot Colorado, 35–12. The Avalanche had four shots in each period.

3 **1993:** Eric Desjardins became the first NHL defenceman to score a hat trick in the Stanley Cup Final. His third goal of the game at 0:51 of OT gave Montreal a 3–2 win over the Kings in Game Two of the Final. It was the Canadiens eighth straight OT win in the playoffs. Desjardins had tied the game with 1:13 remaining. Marty McSorley was in the penalty box for having an illegal curve on his stick.

4 **1980:** 52-year-old Gordie Howe retired for the second and final time, ending his 32-year career as a player after one season with Hartford. Howe retired as the NHL's all-time leader in games (1767), goals (801), assists (1049) and points (1850).

5 **1973:** The Houston Aeros of the World Hockey Association signed Gordie Howe and sons Marty and Mark. It was Gordie's return to professional hockey following his retirement from Detroit after the 1970–71 NHL season.

6 **1996:** Peter Forsberg scored three goals in the first period (his first career playoff hat trick), and Joe Sakic picked up four assists to tie a Stanley Cup Final record as Colorado won 8–1 over visiting Florida in Game Two of the Stanley Cup Final.

7 **1997:** Red Wings beat the Flyers 2–1 in Detroit to win the Stanley Cup in a sweep of the Final. Mike Vernon won the Conn Smythe Trophy and Scotty Bowman became the first coach to win the Cup with three different teams (Montreal, Pittsburgh, Detroit). He also made it to the Cup Final as head coach of the St. Louis Blues.

8 **2000:** Dallas Stars Ed Belfour made 48 saves and Mike Modano scored the lone goal at 6:21 of the third overtime as the Stars beat the Devils 1–0 at New Jersey in Game 5 of the Stanley Cup Final. It was the longest 1–0 game in Cup Final history. Stars had four straight games in the finals with one goal in each.

9 **2001:** Alex Tanguay scored twice and added an assist as the Colorado Avalanche beat the visiting New Jersey Devils 3–1 in Game Seven to win the 2001 Stanley Cup. Patrick Roy won the Conn Smythe Trophy for the third time in his career.

10 **1996:** Patrick Roy made 63 saves for his eighth career playoff shutout, and Uwe Krupp scored the winning goal at 4:31 of the third OT in Game Four as Colorado won 1–0 at Florida to win the Stanley Cup.

11 **1998:** Kris Draper scored at 15:24 of OT to give the Red Wings a 5–4 win over the Capitals, in Game Two of the Stanley Cup Final, in Detroit. Red Wings came back from a two-goal deficit in the third period for their sixth straight win in the Final.

12 **1979:** At 33 years old, Bobby Orr became the youngest player in NHL history to join the Hockey Hall of Fame. Due to bad knees, Orr retired at a young age. He played just 36 games in the final four seasons of his career.

13 **2002:** Brendan Shanahan scored twice as Detroit beat the visiting Carolina Hurricanes 3–1 to win the 2002 Stanley Cup in five games. Scotty Bowman then announced his retirement after becoming the first coach to win nine Stanley Cups.

14 **1994:** Vancouver's Kirk McLean set an NHL record for most minutes played in one playoff year (1,544) as the Canucks lost 3–2 to the Rangers in Game Seven of the Stanley Cup Final. McLean broke Ron Hextall's record of 1540, set with Philadelphia in 1987.

15 **1999:** Dixon Ward scored the winning goal at 7:37 in the second period, and Dominik Hasek made 30 saves in the Sabres 2–1 win against the visiting Dallas Stars, in Game 4 of the Stanley Cup Final.

16 **1998:** Detroit beat the Capitals 4–1 in Game Four for the Red Wings' second straight sweep in the Stanley Cup Final. Steve Yzerman won the Conn Smythe Trophy and Scotty Bowman tied Toe Blake's coaching record with eight Stanley Cups.

17   **1995:** Scotty Bowman became the first coach in NHL history to appear in the Stanley Cup Final with four teams when the Red Wings lost to New Jersey in Game One of the Final. Bowman had previously appeared with St. Louis, Montreal, and Pittsburgh.

18   **1987:** In a unique transaction, the New York Rangers traded their 1988 first-round draft pick to the Quebec Nordiques in exchange for the Nordiques coach Michel Bergeron.

19   **1999:** Brett Hull scored the winning goal at 14:51 of the third overtime and Ed Belfour made 53 saves as Dallas won 2–1 at Buffalo, in Game Six of the Final to win the 1999 Stanley Cup.

20   **1992:** Quebec Nordiques traded the rights to Eric Lindros to both Philadelphia and the New York Rangers, in a trade that was forced to go to arbitration. Eventually Lindros was awarded to Philadelphia.

21   **1999:** The NHL announced new rule changes for regular-season overtime games (starting in 1999–2000): from this point teams would play OT 4-on-4 (skaters) and each team would get one point for the tie, with an additional point going to the overtime winner.

22   **1979:** The Edmonton Oilers, Hartford Whalers, Quebec Nordiques and Winnipeg Jets joined the National Hockey League, as the NHL expanded to 21 teams for the 1979–80 season. The World Hockey Association ceased operation.

23   **1999:** The Hockey Hall of Fame announced it's three newest members: Wayne Gretzky, referee Andy Van Hellemond and Ian "Scotty" Morrison.

24 **1995:** Neal Broten and Shawn Chambers each scored twice as the Devils won 5–2 to sweep the Red Wings in four games and win the 1995 Stanley Cup (for the first time in franchise history). Claude Lemieux was the Conn Smythe Trophy winner.

25 **1997:** The NHL officially approved expansion to a 30-team league by the year 2000, with the announcement of new franchises in Nashville, Atlanta, Columbus and Minnesota.

26 **2004:** The Washington Capitals selected left wing Alexander Ovechkin with the first-overall pick in the 2004 NHL Entry Draft.

27 **1972:** Bobby Hull signed with the Winnipeg Jets of the World Hockey Association for $250,000 a year for 10 years. The signing began the NHL-WHA rivalry. This signing meant that Hull couldn't be a member of Team Canada in the upcoming Summit Series against the Soviet Union.

28 **1964:** Montreal Canadiens made a trade with the Boston Bruins to obtain the rights to amateur goaltender Ken Dryden who was just 16 years old at the time.

29 **1990:** In an exchange of hometown heroes, Chicago traded Montreal native Denis Savard to the Canadiens for Chicago native Chris Chelios.

30 **1992:** After an arbitration victory Philadelphia officially acquired Eric Lindros from the Quebec Nordiques, in exchange for Peter Forsberg, Ron Hextall, Mike Ricci, Steve Duchesne, Kerry Huffman, a 1993 first-round pick (Jocelyn Thibault) and cash.

JULY

1 **1995:** Quebec Nordiques announced that their franchise would be moving to Denver, Colorado. The NHL was returning to Denver after a 13-year absence.

2 **1997:** Dallas Stars signed free agent Eddie Belfour to a three-year, $10 million contract. Belfour had split the 1996–97 season with Chicago and San Jose.

3 **2003:** Dallas Stars named Mike Modano their new captain, replacing Derian Hatcher (who had signed as a free agent with Detroit earlier in the day).

4 **2000:** Toronto Maple Leafs signed free agents Shayne Corson (Canadiens) for three years, $6.75 million and Gary Roberts (Hurricanes) for 3 years, $8 million.

5 **2000:** The NHL named Hall of Fame referee Andy Van Hellemond as the league's new Director of Officiating. Van Hellemond also holds the record for most regular season games (1,475), playoff games (227), and Stanley Cup Final appearances (19).

6 **1978:** The New York Islanders signed John Tonelli as a free agent. Tonelli had been playing in the WHA with the Houston Aeros.

7 **1980:** Veteran goalie Gerry Cheevers announced his retirement as player and was named as the new coach of the Boston Bruins, replacing Harry Sinden. Cheevers would coach the Bruins for the next five seasons.

8 **1995:** In a major trade during the 1995 NHL Entry Draft in Edmonton, the Vancouver Canucks obtained Alexander Mogilny from Buffalo in exchange for Mike Peca, Mike Wilson and their number-one pick (Jay McKee) in the draft held that day. (The draft was held in July because of the lockout that delayed the end of the season.)

9 **1905:** Hall of Famer Clarence Campbell, NHL President 1946 to 1977, was born. The Campbell bowl is given yearly to the team that wins the Eastern Conference in the playoffs.

10 **1957:** Detroit Red Wings obtained goalie Terry Sawchuk from Boston in exchange for Johnny Bucyk and cash. This would be Sawchuk's second stint with the Red Wings and Bucyk would go on to have a Hall of Fame career with the Bruins.

11 **1952:** Hall of Famer Bill Barber was born in Callander, Ontario. Barber played in the NHL from 1972 to 1985 with Philadelphia. Barber also coached the Flyers from 2000 to 2002.

12 **1972:** Team Canada announced their playing roster for the upcoming Summit Series. Thirty-five players were named to the team's training camp.

13 **2000:** New York Rangers announced the re-signing of free agent Mark Messier to a two-year, $11 million contract. Messier had spent the previous three years with Vancouver.

14 **1989:** Quebec Nordiques signed free agent Guy Lafleur after his one-year comeback with the New York Rangers. The Rangers received Quebec's fifth-round pick (Sergei Zubov) in the 1990 Entry Draft as compensation.

15 **1997:** Colorado Avalanche coach Marc Crawford was named head coach of the 1998 Canadian Olympic team, scheduled to play in Nagano, Japan. Philadelphia head coach Wayne Cashman was named as his assistant.

16 **1988:** Wayne Gretzky married actress Janet Jones in Edmonton at St. Joseph's Basilica. It would be the last ring Gretzky would put on in Edmonton, as he was traded two months later.

17 **1989:** Bob Gainey left the Montreal Canadiens after 16 seasons to become player-coach of the Epinal Squirrels, a division-two team in France. He left as third all-time in Canadiens games played (1,160).

18 **1997:** Ken Holland was named the new general manager of the Detroit Red Wings and Scotty Bowman signed a two-year extension to continue as coach of the team.

19 **1892:** Hall of Fame coach Dick Irvin, who won four Stanley Cups during his coaching career, was born in Limestone Ridge, Ontario.

20 **1972:** Montreal Canadiens defenceman J.C. Tremblay signed a five-year contract with the Quebec Nordiques of the newly formed World Hockey Association. Tremblay had played 794 games with the Canadiens. Maurice Richard was hired as the team's first head coach.

21 **1996:** New York Rangers announced the signing of free agent Wayne Gretzky. Gretzky and Mario Lemieux would tie for the league lead in assists that season with 72.

22 **2003:** In a three-way trade, Columbus sent centre Mike Sillinger and a second-round draft pick in 2004 to Dallas for defenceman Darryl Sydor. The Stars then traded Sillinger with a conditional draft pick to Phoenix for defenceman Teppo Numminen.

23 **1957:** In one of hockey's biggest trades, Detroit sent Ted Lindsay and Glenn Hall to Chicago in exchange for Johnny Wilson, Hank Bassen, Forbes Kennedy and Bob Preston. Lindsay had been captain of the Red Wings from 1952 to 1956 and he led the NHL in assists (55) in 1956–57.

24 **2003:** L.A. Kings signed free agent Luc Robitaille (Red Wings) to a one-year contract, for his third tour of duty with the team.

25 **1977:** Toronto Maple Leafs named Roger Neilson as their new head coach, replacing Red Kelly. Neilson would coach the Leafs for two seasons. He was inducted into the Hockey Hall of Fame as a builder in 2002 and passed away in June of 2003.

26 **1989:** L.A. Kings signed free agent veteran defenceman Larry Robinson to a three-year contract. Robinson had spent 17 seasons with Montreal.

27 **1988:** Frank Zamboni, the inventor of the ice-cleaning machine that coincidentally enough has his name on it, passed away at the age of 87 in Paramount, California.

28 **1998:** Veteran defenceman Viacheslav Fetisov, one of the first Soviet stars to play in the NHL, announced his retirement. Fetisov would return to the New Jersey Devils as an assistant coach.

29 **1934:** Didier Pitre, the first player signed by the Montreal Canadiens, died at the age of 50. He had 60 goals in his first 83 NHL games.

30 **1998:** Veteran defenceman Kevin Lowe announced his retirement, after 19 seasons in the NHL with the Oilers and the Rangers. He started his new career as an assistant coach with the Rangers.

31 **2000:** Tampa Bay Lightning signed Martin St. Louis (Flames) as a free agent to a two-year, $525,000 contract. St. Louis had two uneventful seasons in Calgary.

AUGUST

1 **1997:** Mighty Ducks of Anaheim announced the signing of free agent Tomas Sandstrom. He had just won a Stanley Cup with Detroit that spring. Sandstrom would play two seasons with the Ducks before departing for Sweden to finish his career.

2 **1999:** Chicago Blackhawks signed unrestricted free agent Wendel Clark (Red Wings) to a one-year contract. Clark was released by the Blackhawks in November.

3 **1951:** Hall of Famer Marcel Dionne was born in Drummondville, Quebec. Dionne played in the NHL from 1971 to 1989 with Detroit, L.A. and the New York Rangers.

4 **1921:** Hall of Famer Maurice Richard, the first player to score 50 goals in 50 games, was born in Montreal. Richard played in the NHL from 1942 to 1960 with Montreal.

5   **1996:** San Jose Sharks signed free agent Bernie Nicholls, who had spent the previous season with Chicago. Despite having scored 70 goals with the Kings, Nicholls would score just 18 goals in over two seasons with the Sharks.

6   **2004:** Phoenix Coyotes announced the signing of free agent Brett Hull (Red Wings) to a two-year contract. Due to the lockout, he played just five games with the Coyotes, all in October 2005. He scored no goals.

7   **1992:** Chicago Blackhawks traded goalie Dominik Hasek to Buffalo, in exchange for Sabres goalie Stephane Beauregard and a fourth-round draft choice (Eric Daze) in 1993.

8   **1991:** Wendel Clark was named the 14th captain in Toronto Maple Leafs history, replacing Rob Ramage. Clark would spend three seasons as captain before being traded to the Nordiques in the summer of 1994.

9   **1988:** In hockey's biggest trade ever, Edmonton sent Wayne Gretzky, Mike Krushelnyski and Marty McSorley to the L.A. Kings in exchange for Jimmy Carson, Martin Gelinas, three first round draft choices (1989 traded to Devils; 1991, Martin Rucinsky; 1993 Nick Stajduhar) and cash.

10   **1994:** Dallas Stars were awarded Peter Zezel and Grant Marshall as compensation from Toronto for the Maple Leafs signing of free agent Mike Craig.

11   **1958:** NHL centre Ken "The Rat" Linseman was born in Kingston, Ontario. Linseman played in the NHL from 1978 to 1992 with Philadelphia, Edmonton, Boston and Toronto.

12   **1981:** Serge Savard announced his retirement after a 17-year NHL career with Montreal and the Winnipeg Jets. Savard was inducted into the Hockey Hall of Fame in 1986.

13 **1949:** Hall of Famer Bobby Clarke was born in Flin Flon, Manitoba. Clarke played in the NHL from 1969 to 1984 with the Philadelphia Flyers.

14 **1996:** Anaheim signs 36-year-old free agent Jari Kurri to a contract. Kurri spent the previous season with the Kings and Rangers. He entered the 1996–97 season with 583 career goals. He wouldn't reach 600 until 1997–98.

15 **1989:** Toronto fired head coach George Armstrong. Odd time of year to fire a coach. Was he due a bonus on August 16? In 1967, Armstrong had scored the infamous empty net goal to seal the Leafs' last Stanley Cup win.

16 **1996:** Phoenix Coyotes obtained Jeremy Roenick from Chicago, in exchange for Alexei Zhamnov, Craig Mills and the Coyotes 1997 first-round draft choice (Ty Jones).

17 **1992:** Bryan Trottier retired from the NHL as a player to join the New York Islanders front office. Trottier had led the NHL in scoring in 1978–79 with the Islanders. He would be inducted into the Hockey Hall of Fame in 1997.

18 **1994:** Toronto Maple Leafs named Doug Gilmour as their new captain, the 15th in team history. He replaced Wendel Clark (who had been traded to the Quebec Nordiques).

19 **1988:** New York Rangers signed 37-year-old Guy Lafleur to a one-year contract. Lafleur had been elected to the Hockey Hall of Fame two and a half months earlier. He went on to score 18 goals and 27 assists in 67 games that year.

20 **1926:** Boston Bruins purchased Eddie Shore from the Edmonton Eskimos of the Western Hockey League. Shore would win four Hart Trophies with the Bruins and was inducted into the Hockey Hall of Fame in 1947.

Old-time hockey. Four-time Hart Memorial Trophy winner Eddie Shore signs a kid's stick. PHOTO: COURTESY OF THE BOSTON PUBLIC LIBRARY, LESLIE JONES COLLECTION

21 **1912:** Hall of Famer Toe Blake was born in Victoria Mines, Ontario. Blake played in the NHL from 1934 to 1948 with the Montreal Canadiens and the Montreal Maroons.

22 **2001:** Detroit Red Wings signed unrestricted free agent Brett Hull, who had been with the Dallas Stars. Hull won the Stanley Cup with the famous foot in the crease goal versus Buffalo in 1999. The Golden Brett would score 741 goals in his NHL career.

23 **1976:** Minnesota North Stars traded goaltender Cesare Maniago to Vancouver in exchange for Gary Smith. With the North Stars in 1968–69, Maniago had led the NHL in losses, 34, and most goals against, 134.

24 **1980:** Peter Stastny and his brother Anton left the national team of Czechoslovakia at Innsbruck, Austria, after a 4–3 loss to the USSR. They left at midnight and defected to Canada. Their brother Marian would later join them.

25 **1997:** Neal Broten, the final member of the gold medal–winning 1980 U.S. Olympic hockey team to play in the NHL, announced his retirement after 17 NHL seasons.

26 **1998:** Mike Gartner (at that time, the fifth all-time in career NHL goal scoring) retired after 19 seasons in the league. Gartner scored 708 goals, 627 assists and 1,335 career points, the 18th in NHL history at the time of his retirement.

27 **1974:** Detroit obtained 1969 Calder Trophy winner Danny Grant from the Minnesota North Stars, in exchange for Henry Boucha.

28 **1989:** Just three months after winning the Stanley Cup, Lanny McDonald announced his retirement after 16 years in the NHL.

29 **1994:** Pittsburgh's Mario Lemieux announced that he would sit out the 1994–95 NHL season due to fatigue from his battle with cancer. He returned in 1995–96 and won the NHL's Art Ross Trophy as the league's leading scorer.

30 **1994:** Montreal Canadiens named Kirk Muller as their new team captain, the 20th in team history. Muller replaced Guy Carbonneau, who had been traded to St. Louis.

31 **1931:** Hall of Famer Jean Beliveau was born in Trois-Rivières, Quebec. Beliveau played his entire NHL career, from 1950 to 1971, with Montreal.

SEPTEMBER

1 **1999:** Pittsburgh Penguins became the first club in pro-hockey history to be owned by a former member of the team, when Mario Lemieux assumed ownership of the Penguins.

2 **1972:** The Soviet Union defeated Team Canada 7–3 in Montreal, in Game One of the historic 1972 Summit Series. It was a rough start for Canada as most had thought Canada would win all eight games of series. Bobby Orr was out with an injury and Bobby Hull was not on team because he left NHL for WHA.

3 **1966:** Bobby Orr signed his first NHL contract with the Boston Bruins, a two-year deal paying $70,000 plus a signing bonus, the top salary in the league.

4 **1972:** Team Canada defeated the Soviet Union 4–1 in Toronto in Game Two of the Summit Series. It was Canada's only win on home soil in the series. Canada, at all levels of play, has never lost in Toronto.

5   **1946:** Clarence Campbell was named the new president of the NHL. He was probably best remembered for suspending Maurice Richard for the remainder of the 1954–55 season for punching a linesman on March 13th. A few days later the Richard Riots ensued in Montreal, with Campbell in attendance.

6   **1972:** Canada and the Soviet Union tied 4–4 in Winnipeg in Game Three of the Summit Series with Bobby Hull watching from the stands.

7   **1945:** Hall of Famer Jacques Lemaire was born in LaSalle, Quebec. Lemaire played in the NHL from 1967 to 1979 with Montreal and later coached the team.

8   **1972:** The Soviet Union defeated Canada 5–3 in Vancouver, in the final game in Canada of the Summit Series. Following the game Phil Esposito had his legendary speech about the fans booing the team.

9   **1971:** Gordie Howe announced his retirement as an active NHL player. His new title was vice-president with the Detroit Red Wings. He came out of retirement two years later to join the World Hockey Association.

10   **1943:** Toronto obtained the rights to Ted Kennedy from Montreal in exchange for the rights to Frank Eddolls. Kennedy would spend his entire 696-game NHL career with Toronto.

11   **1993:** Toronto Maple Leafs and New York Rangers met in the first of two exhibition games at Wembley Arena in London, England. Rangers outscored the Leafs in the first game, 5–3, and the second, 3–1, winning both games of the "French's Mustard Cup."

12 **1985:** Pittsburgh traded Marty McSorley and future considerations, which turned out to be Craig Muni, to Edmonton along with Tim Hrynewich in exchange for Gilles Meloche.

13 **1987:** Mario Lemieux scored at 10:07 of the second OT to give Team Canada a 6–5 win over the Soviet Union and the title in the best-of-three Canada Cup final.

14 **1979:** Edmonton Oilers signed free agent defenceman Charlie Huddy, undrafted from the Oshawa Generals. Huddy went on to win five Stanley Cups as a member of the Oilers.

15 **1960:** Maurice Richard announced his NHL retirement at the Queen Elizabeth Hotel in Montreal after a career that saw him score a team-record 544 regular season goals along with 82 playoff goals.

16 **1978:** Seventeen-year-old Wayne Gretzky attended his first pro training camp, as a member of the WHA's Indianapolis Racers.

17 **1971:** Montreal's Guy Lafleur made his NHL debut and picked up three assists in the Canadiens' 7–4 exhibition game victory against the Bruins at the Forum.

18 **1998:** Eighteen months after being found to have cancer, John Cullen began his NHL comeback by scoring the game–winning goal in the Tampa Bay Lightning's 3–1 win over the Buffalo Sabres, in a pre-season game played in Innsbruck, Austria.

19 **1992:** Eric Lindros made his NHL debut with a goal and an assist in the Flyers 4–3 win over the Quebec Nordiques (the team Lindros refused to play for) in an exhibition game before a crowd of 17,226 disgruntled fans. Some wore baby outfits.

20 **1995:** Toronto Maple Leafs signed free agent Wayne Gretzky's younger brother Brent (Lightning). Brent would spend the season with Toronto's AHL affiliate in St. John's, Newfoundland.

21 **1967:** Goatender Jacques Plante (who had retired from the NHL after the 1964–65 season) played goal for the California Seals in an exhibition game against the L.A. Kings, in Port Huron, Michigan. The game ended in a 3–3 tie.

22 **1972:** Team Canada lost the first European-hosted game of the historic Summit Series in Moscow, 5–4. It was Game Five of the series.

23 **1992:** Manon Rheaume became the first woman to play in an NHL exhibition game when she played in goal for the Lightning. She made seven saves and gave up two goals in one period in a game against the Blues, in Tampa Bay. Brendan Shanahan scored one of the goals.

24 **1972:** Team Canada defeated the Soviet Union 3–2 in Moscow in Game Six of the Summit Series. Paul Henderson scored the game-winning goal.

25 **1926:** The NHL officially granted franchises to two new teams: Chicago Black Hawks and Detroit Cougars (later the Falcons, then the Red Wings) raising the NHL total to ten teams.

26 **1972:** Phil Esposito scored twice, and Paul Henderson scored the game winner at 17:54 of the final period to give Team Canada a 4–3 win over the Soviet Union in Game Seven of the 1972 Summit Series.

27 **1991:** The L.A. Kings defeated the New York Rangers before a crowd of 13,000 in an exhibition game played outdoors at Caesar's Palace Hotel in Las Vegas. The warm temperatures and shadows on the ice made play difficult.

28 **1972:** Paul Henderson scored his third-straight game-winning goal with 34 seconds remaining in the game to give Team Canada a 6–5 win over the Soviets in Moscow in Game 8 of the historic Summit Series.

29 **1997:** St. Louis Blues named 22-year-old Chris Pronger as their new team captain, the 16th (and youngest) captain in Blues history.

30 **1997:** Toronto Maple Leafs named Mats Sundin as their new Team Captain, 16th in team history and the first European-born.

OCTOBER

1 **1999:** Edmonton Oilers retired Wayne Gretzky's #99 jersey in an Opening Night pre-game ceremony, prior to a 1–1 tie against the visiting New York Rangers. Ryan Smyth scored for the Oilers.

2 **1999:** Boston's Ray Bourque became the defenceman with the most career goals in NHL history when his 386th goal moved him one ahead of Paul Coffey. The milestone came in a 3–1 Bruins loss to the visiting Carolina Hurricanes.

3 **1953:** Jean Beliveau signed his first contract with the Montreal Canadiens and was assigned #4 for the first time in his NHL career (after having worn #17, #20 and #12 during previous brief stays with the Canadiens).

4 **1962:** In Dr. Evil–like fashion the Chicago Black Hawks offered Toronto $1 million for left winger Frank Mahovlich. The Maple Leafs eventually refused the deal. Mahovlich finished the 1961–62 season second in goals (33) and fifth in points (71).

5 **1983:** Edmonton Oilers centre Wayne Gretzky scored a goal and added an assist during a 5–4 win over Toronto in the 1983–84 season opener. It was the beginning of an NHL-record 51-game scoring streak for Gretzky that lasted until January 28, 1984.

6 **1988:** Wayne Gretzky scored his first goal in a Kings uniform on his first shot of the game, as the Kings won on their opening night, 8–2 over Detroit. Gretzky had a goal and three assists in the game and passed 83 Kings for the team's all-time scoring, including John Gibson (0 points), not related.

7 **1976:** Chicago's Stan Mikita became just the third player in NHL history to score 1,300 career points. The milestone came with his one goal in a 6–5 Black Hawks win over the Blues in St. Louis.

8 **1975:** Doug Jarvis played the first of his NHL-record 964 consecutive games (over a span of 12 years). Jarvis started with Montreal, continued the streak with the Capitals and ended it with Hartford on Oct. 10, 1987 in a game against the Rangers where he was a healthy scratch.

9 **1986:** L.A. Kings centre Marcel Dionne became just the second player in NHL history (along with Gordie Howe) to score 1,600 NHL points, when he picked up two assists in a 4–3 loss to St. Louis.

10 **1995:** St. Louis' Brett Hull scored four goals for the second time in his career as St. Louis won 5–3 over the visiting Oilers. It was the 24th hat trick of Hull's NHL career. All four goals came against Bill Ranford.

11 **1984:** In his first NHL game, in his first shift, on his first shot, Penguins rookie Mario Lemieux scored his first NHL goal on Pete Peeters (goalie so good, they named him twice), and later added an assist. Nevertheless, the Penguins lost 4–3 to the Bruins in their season opener at Boston.

12 **1980:** Toronto's Wilf Paiement scored an empty-net goal in a 4–2 Maple Leafs win at Philadelphia for the 100,000th goal in NHL history. It came in the NHL's 64th season of existence. Phil Myre was Philadelphia's goalie on the bench.

13 **1947:** Toronto Maple Leafs faced a group of NHL All-Stars in the first game featuring the Stanley Cup champions against a group of All-Stars from the rest of the league. The All-Stars won 4–3 in a benefit for the players' pension fund. It was the first NHL All-Star game since 1939.

14 **1979:** Wayne Gretzky scored his first NHL goal a 4–4 tie between the Canucks and the Oilers in Edmonton. Glen Hanlon was the victim of Gretzky's first NHL goal in the third game of the season.

15 **1989:** Wayne Gretzky picked up a first-period assist for career point number 1,850 to tie Gordie Howe, then scored in the final minute to become the NHL's all-time leading point scorer. He scored again in OT to lead the Kings to a 5–4 win at Edmonton.

16   **1988:** Guy Lafleur scored his first goal in three years, 11 months and 22 days. It was his first goal as a New York Ranger. He also added an assist and led the Rangers to a 3–2 win over the Canucks at Madison Square Garden.

17   **2000:** Patrick Roy set an NHL record for most wins by a goaltender, breaking Terry Sawchuk's record of 447, as Colorado won 4–3 in overtime at Washington.

18   **1977:** Rogie Vachon made 43 saves to earn his 43rd career shutout and Glenn Resch had 28 saves for his 15th career shutout in a scoreless tie between the Kings and Islanders at Long Island. It was the first scoreless tie in Islanders' history.

19   **1966:** Detroit's Gordie Howe played in the first game of his 21st consecutive season in the NHL, breaking the old league record of 20 years, held by Dit Clapper and Bill Gadsby. He picked up an assist in a 6–2 loss at Boston.

20   **1977:** Indianapolis Racers rookie Wayne Gretzky scored his first two pro-hockey goals, in a 4–3 loss to Edmonton. The goals came in Gretzky's second career WHA game.

21   **1993:** NHL history was made in Detroit when Paul Devorski was the referee in a game in which his younger brother Greg was a linesman, the first-ever NHL game to feature brothers as on-ice officials. The Wings won the game 6–2 over the Winnipeg Jets.

22   **1988:** Mario Lemieux scored two goals and added two assists, Paul Coffey picked up four assists and Tom Barrasso tied his own NHL record for goalies with an assist in his third straight game as the Penguins won 7–4 against the visiting Chicago Blackhawks.

23 **1965:** Chicago's Bobby Hull scored an opening-night hat trick (the 14th of his career), and Glenn Hall recorded his 63rd career shutout in the Black Hawks' 4–0 win at Toronto. Hull went on to lead the NHL in 1965–66 with a record 54 goals in 70 games.

The Golden Jet, Bobby Hull, shocked the hockey world when he left the NHL to play in the WHA in 1972. PHOTO: LIBRARY AND ARCHIVES CANADA/ CREDIT: LOUIS JAQUES/WEEKEND MAGAZINE FONDS/E002505660

24 **1974:** L.A. Kings were outshot 55–31 by Buffalo, but Rogie Vachon made 53 saves and Don Kozak scored his second career hat trick (plus two assists) to lead them to a 7–2 win over the Sabres, at the Forum.

25 **1984:** Guy Lafleur scored his 518th and final goal as a member of the Montreal Canadiens in a 3–2 win over Buffalo. His next NHL goal would come four years later with the New York Rangers.

26 **1990:** Wayne Gretzky became the first player in NHL history to hit the 2,000-point milestone. He got one assist as the Kings lost 6–2 to the Jets at Winnipeg. He upped his career stats to 684 goals and 1,316 assists for 2,000 points in 857 NHL games.

27 **1968:** Gordie Howe became the first player in NHL history to get 900 career assists and 600 career goals, when he picked up three assists in the Red Wings 7–5 win over the visiting Boston Bruins.

28 **1993:** Toronto Maple Leafs extended their NHL record to ten-straight wins from the start of the season with a 4–2 win over the Blackhawks at Chicago.

29 **2003:** Pittsburgh's Mario Lemieux became the sixth player in NHL history to reach 1,700 career points (and the second fastest, after Gretzky) with an assist in a 4–4 tie against the visiting New York Islanders.

30 **1983:** The Sutter brothers made NHL history when the Islanders played in Philadelphia. New York's Duane and Brent and the Flyers' twins Rich and Ron became the first four brothers to play in the same NHL game. Islanders won the game 6–2.

31 **1987:** New York Rangers' centre Marcel Dionne scored the 700th goal of his NHL career, joining Gordie Howe (801) and Phil Esposito (717) as the only players at the time to reach that plateau. The goal came in an 8–2 loss to the Islanders.

NOVEMBER

1 **1959:** Jacques Plante became the first goalie to wear a mask on a full-time basis after taking a slapshot to the face by the Rangers' Andy Bathgate.

2 **1937:** An All-Star game (the second in NHL history) was held at the Forum in Montreal as a benefit for the family of recently deceased Howie Morenz. A crowd of 8,683 were on hand as the NHL All-Stars defeated a combined team of Canadiens and Montreal Maroons, 6–5.

3 **1993:** Ottawa rookie Alexei Yashin set a Senators team record for most points in a game with three goals (his first career hat trick) and two assists in a 7–5 win against the Oilers at Edmonton.

4 **1987:** Edmonton Oilers beat Rangers 7–2 as Wayne Gretzky of the Oilers and Marcel Dionne of the Rangers both entered the game with 998 career assists. Gretzky got two to become the second NHL player to get 1,000 while Dionne picked up one assist for 999.

5 **1983:** Rangers and Nordiques set an NHL record for the fastest two goals at the start of a period by two teams (14 seconds). Andre Savard scored for Quebec at 0:08 of the third and Pierre Larouche replied for the Rangers at 0:14. The game ended in a 4–4 tie.

6 **1995:** Rangers' Mark Messier scored his 17th career hat trick in the final period to reach the 500-goal mark and added an assist as New York won 4–2 over the Flames in New York. Messier became the 21st player in the NHL to collect 500 goals.

7 **1995:** Toronto's Larry Murphy picked up three assists to get 961 NHL career points, passing Larry Robinson and moving into fourth on the all-time scoring list for defenceman (behind Paul Coffey, Ray Bourque and Denis Potvin). Leafs won 6–3 over Anaheim.

8 **1978:** Bobby Orr announced his retirement from the NHL at a news conference in Chicago. His final career totals were 270 goals, 645 assists, 915 points in 657 games.

9 **2000:** Roman Cechmanek became the first goaltender since 1938 to get each of his first two victories as shutouts, in the Flyers 2–0 win against the visiting Edmonton Oilers. He had picked up his first victory (and shutout) five nights earlier.

10 **1999:** Steve Yzerman became the NHL's all-time leader in points among players who spent their entire careers with one team. His 12th of the year (in a 4–2 Red Wings victory at Dallas) gave him 1,495 career points, one more than Mario Lemieux.

11 **2002:** Dave Andreychuk scored the 249th power-play goal of his career to tie Phil Esposito's NHL record as Tampa Bay won 4–2 over the visiting Phoenix Coyotes.

12 **1989:** New York Rangers exploded for 26 shots in the second period (and 45 in the game) en route to a 4–2 win over the Islanders at Madison Square Garden.

13 **1947:** For the first time in NHL history, the league initiated the policy of having players raise their sticks to signify the scoring of a goal. Montreal's Billy Reay became the first to do so as the Canadiens beat Chicago 5–2 at the Forum.

14 **2001:** Patrick Roy became the first goaltender in NHL history to win 200 games with two teams (Montreal and Colorado) when the Avalanche won 1–0 against the visiting Minnesota Wild. It was Roy's 54th career shutout.

15 **2002:** Patrick Roy became the NHL career leader in minutes played, passing Terry Sawchuk as the Avalanche lost 4–2 to the Stars at Dallas.

16 **1986:** New York Islanders' Mike Bossy scored the 545th goal of his career and surpassed Hall of Famer Maurice Richard to move into sixth place on the NHL's all-time scoring list. Islanders lost 3–1 to the Jets at Winnipeg.

17 **1990:** Steve Yzerman scored three goals (on three shots) in the first 12 minutes of the game (for his 10th career hat trick), then added two assists, to lead the Red Wings to an 8–4 win at Toronto.

18 **2001:** Patrick Roy recorded his third consecutive shutout (the 56th of his career) and Rob Blake ended a 12-game goal-less streak with two goals as the Avalanche won 2–0 against the Devils at New Jersey.

19 **1966:** Rookie Bobby Orr received his first NHL major penalty after a fight with Vic Hadfield of the Rangers in a game in Boston that ended in a 3–3 tie.

20 **1974:** Toronto's Dave Keon played in his 1,000th career NHL game and scored his fifth career hat trick, as the Maple Leafs lost 8–5 to the Pittsburgh Penguins. Keon became the third player to appear in 1,000 games with Toronto along with George Armstrong (1,187) and Tim Horton (1,185). Borje Salming (1,099) and Ron Ellis (1,034) would also join this group in their careers.

21 **1992:** Quebec Nordiques just missed setting an NHL record with four goals in a span of one minute and 33 seconds in the second period of an 8–2 win over the Hartford Whalers in Quebec City. Boston holds the NHL record with four goals in one minute and 20 seconds, set in 1945.

22 **2003:** Montreal Canadiens beat the Oilers 4–3 at the first outdoor game in NHL history, played before a record crowd of 57,167 fans in Edmonton.

23 **1988:** Wayne Gretzky scored a goal and five assists to become the fifth player in NHL history to score 600 goals, as the Kings won 8–3 at Detroit. Gretzky followed Howe, Esposito, Dionne and Hull in the 600 club, but he scored his in just 718 games.

24 **1989:** Mario Lemieux improved his career penalty-shot record to a perfect five-for-five when he scored against Bob Mason in a 7–4 Penguins' win at Washington.

25 **1988:** Pittsburgh Penguins beat Washington 5–3 in a game where all eight goals were scored by special teams. Pittsburgh had four power-play goals and one shorthanded tally, while the Capitals had three power-play goals.

26 **2003:** Scott Stevens set an NHL record for defenceman by playing in his 1,616th career NHL game (breaking the record held by Larry Murphy) as the Devils tied 3–3 against the Mighty Ducks in Anaheim.

27 **1965:** Detroit's Gordie Howe scored his 600th NHL goal. It came in a 6–2 Red Wings loss to Montreal. Howe also got a major penalty that night for elbowing J.C. Tremblay. Howe became the first NHL player to get 600 career goals.

28 **1979:** Billy Smith became the first goalie in NHL history to get credit for a goal. He was the last Islander to touch the puck before Rob Ramage of Colorado put it into his own net. But the Islanders lost 7–4 to the Rockies at Denver.

29 **1984:** Playing in his 416th NHL game, Edmonton's Wayne Gretzky recorded his 599th and 600th career assists as the Oilers won 4–2 at Boston.

30 **1968:** St. Louis goalie Glenn Hall recorded the 75th shutout of his NHL career in the Blues' 1–0 win over the visiting Philadelphia Flyers. The win gave the Blues a team-record nine-game unbeaten streak (5–0–4).

DECEMBER

1 **1996:** Rangers' Wayne Gretzky became the first player in NHL history to reach the 3,000-point plateau (including playoffs) with an assist in a 6–2 win over the Canadiens at Madison Square Garden.

2 **2001:** Ed Belfour tied an NHL record (held by Tom Barrasso) by picking up an assist in his third straight game, and he set a Dallas franchise record for goaltenders with his fourth assist of the season, in an 4–2 win at Vancouver.

3 **1972:** Toronto goaltender Jacques Plante got a shutout in the Maple Leafs' 3–0 win at Detroit. It was the 80th career shutout for Plante.

4 **1978:** Kings' centre Marcel Dionne scored his 20th goal of the season, in the Kings' 23rd game of the season (a team record for fastest 20 goals). It came in the Kings' 10–2 win over the Capitals at Forum.

5 **1968:** Montreal's rookie goaltender Tony Esposito made his first NHL start, and gave up two goals to brother Phil, in a 2–2 tie between the Canadiens and the Bruins in Boston Garden.

6 **1999:** Toronto's Steve Thomas set an NHL record with his 10th career regular-season overtime goal when he scored at 1:05 of OT in a 3–2 Maple Leafs win over the Buffalo Sabres. Thomas broke the record of nine OT goals held by Mario Lemieux.

7 **1977:** New England Whalers' Gordie Howe scored his 1,000th professional goal (counting the NHL and WHA) in a WHA Whalers' game against the Birmingham Bulls.

8 **2001:** Calgary Flames set an NHL record by picking up 190 penalty minutes during the third period of a 4–0 loss to the visiting Mighty Ducks. Calgary had a total of 202 penalty minutes in the game The teams combined for 309 penalty minutes in the game.

9 **1982:** Flyers' rookie Ron Sutter made NHL history when he scored his first NHL goal. This was the first time in league history that five brothers from the same family—he joined Duane, Darryl, Brent and Brian—all scored a goal in the NHL. Ron's was the game winner in a 4–1 win over the Quebec Nordiques. His twin brother Rich had not yet scored an NHL goal. He would do that in the 1983–84 season.

10 **1986:** Edmonton's Wayne Gretzky became the first NHL player to score 40 career hat tricks, when his three goals led the Oilers to a 7–4 win against the Jets at Winnipeg.

11 **1977:** Tom Bladon set an NHL record for most points in a game by a defenceman. His eight points (four goals and four assists) led Philadelphia to an 11–1 win over the Cleveland Barons. Bladon also set a record by going plus-10.

12 **1986:** Wayne Gretzky picked up his 900th, 901st and 902nd career assists (in his 584th NHL game) as the Oilers beat the Winnipeg Jets, 6–1.

13 **1997:** Vancouver's Gino Odjick became the fifth NHL player to accumulate 2,000 career penalty minutes with one team, in the Canucks 5–2 loss to Colorado. Odjick joined Boston's Terry O'Reilly, Montreal's Chris Nilan, New Jersey's Ken Daneyko and Buffalo's Rob Ray.

14 **1929:** Toronto's Harold "Baldy" Cotton scored two goals in overtime as the Leafs won 7–6 over the visiting New York Rangers, who had become the first team in NHL history to travel by air (via a charter flight) to face an opponent.

15 **1995:** Winnipeg's 19-year-old rookie defenceman Deron Quint scored two goals in four seconds in the second period to tie a 64-year-old NHL record set by Nels Stewart of the 1931 Montreal Maroons. Jets won 9–4 against the visiting Oilers.

16 **2002:** Montreal's Doug Gilmour became just the 14th player in NHL history to get 1,400 career points, when he scored a goal to help the Canadiens to a 3–2 win at Ottawa.

17   **1983:** In his 352nd career NHL game, Edmonton's Wayne Gretzky scored a goal and added five assists to reach the 500-assist mark and the 800-point mark in his NHL career. Oilers won 8–1 over the visiting Quebec Nordiques.

18   **1954:** Montreal's Maurice Richard became the first player in NHL history to score 400 career goals, when the Canadiens defeated the Black Hawks 4–2 at Chicago.

19   **1970:** Toronto goaltender Jacques Plante recorded his 75th NHL career shutout as the Maple Leafs won 2–0 over the visiting Buffalo Sabres.

20   **1981:** Winnipeg's Doug Smail set an NHL record (later tied by Bryan Trottier and Alex Mogilny) for fastest goal from the start of a game, with a goal just five seconds into the Jets' 5–4 win over St. Louis.

21   **1972:** Boston's Bobby Orr had an assist to set a new NHL record for career points (541) by a defenceman. It came in Orr's 423rd career NHL game, an 8–1 win over Detroit. Doug Harvey held the previous record with 540 points in 1,113 games.

22   **1996:** St. Louis' Brett Hull became part of the first father-son combo to each score 500 career goals, when his 26th career hat trick led the Blues to a 7–4 win over the visiting L.A. Kings. Brett also picked up an assist.

23   **1978:** Bryan Trottier set an NHL record with six points in the second period, and finished the night with five goals and three assists in a 9–4 Islanders' win over the Rangers; the Islanders extended their home undefeated streak to 16 games (12–0–4).

24 **1969:** Mike Walton picked up four assists as the Maple Leafs won 8–1 over the visiting L.A. Kings. NHL used to have a tradition of playing on Christmas Eve and Christmas Day, which came to an end in 1972. Now the NHL takes a three day Christmas break.

25 **1971:** Ken Hodge scored a goal and added three assists to lead Boston to a 5–1 win over the visiting Philadelphia Flyers. This was the final Christmas Day game played by the Bruins.

26 **2001:** Colorado's Patrick Roy became the first goaltender in NHL history to record 500 career wins, and picked up his 59th career shutout, in a 2–0 Avalanche victory at Dallas.

27 **2000:** Mario Lemieux returned from a three-and-a-half-year retirement and picked up a point on his first shift, finishing the night with a goal and two assists in the Penguins 5–0 win against the visiting Toronto Maple Leafs. Garth Snow got the shutout.

28 **1975:** New York Rangers became the first team in NHL history to face a touring Soviet hockey squad. The Soviet Army beat the Rangers 7–3 at Madison Square Garden. Phil Esposito had a goal and two assists for New York.

29 **1995:** Detroit's Scotty Bowman became the NHL's all-time leader in games coached, with his record-setting 1,607th game. He broke the record held by Al Arbour, as the Red Wings won 2–1 at Dallas. Bowman improved his record to 939–428–240.

30 **1989:** Maple Leafs scored six goals in a row to beat Boston 7–6 in overtime and end a seven-game losing streak. Wendel Clark won it at 3:19 of OT. Toronto trailed 6–1 with a minute remaining in the second period.

31 **1955:** Maurice Richard scored the 3,000th goal in Montreal Canadiens' history in the first period. It was assisted by his brother Henri, and Jean Beliveau. The Rocket added two assists in what would be a 7–3 win over the visiting Chicago Black Hawks.

CUE THE VON TRAPP FAMILY SINGERS AND THAT GOODBYE song. So long, farewell, *auf wiedersehen*, good night. That's all I remember...Christopher Plummer—a good Canadian.